HENRY WADSWORTH LONGFELLOW

Portrait of an American Humanist

EDWARD WAGENKNECHT

> The Intelligentsia of today are all wrong about Long-
> fellow, holding him as the very nadir of everything
> that they themselves have not so much sprung from as
> *away* from; he was in some respects the most important
> poet we ever had.
>
> Mary Austin: *Earth Horizon* (1932)

NEW YORK OXFORD UNIVERSITY PRESS 1966

COPYRIGHT © 1955, 1966, BY EDWARD WAGENKNECHT

LIBRARY OF CONGRESS CATALOGUE CARD NUMBER: 66-13267

PRINTED IN THE UNITED STATES OF AMERICA

Once more, for David, and now for Patricia also

PREFACE

My *Longfellow: A Full-Length Portrait* was published by Long-mans, Green & Co. in 1955. It was—and it remains—the only modern book on Longfellow which both covers his entire life and is based upon an exhaustive examination of materials in print and in manuscript. It was allowed to go out of print while there was still considerable demand for it, and today it is practically unobtainable even on the antiquarian market. I have therefore welcomed the desire of Oxford University Press to have a book on Longfellow in the series of portraits of American writers which I am doing for them.

Since 1955 the late Newton Arvin has given Longfellow's poems the most detailed critical examination they have ever been accorded in *Longfellow: His Life and Work* (Atlantic-Little, Brown, 1963). Though Arvin sometimes seems hypercritical, he shows a marked tendency to return with one hand what the other has taken away, as when having definitely classified Longfellow as "a minor writer," he goes on to wipe out the distinction be-tween major and minor as "at best a rough-and-ready one," thus leaving us pretty much where we were before. Less detailed but very intelligent evaluations of Longfellow's poetic achievement have also been made by Edward Hirsh, *Henry Wadsworth Long-fellow*, in the "University of Minnesota Pamphlets on American Writers," No. 35 (University of Minnesota Press, 1964), and by Howard Nemerov, in his introduction to the Longfellow volume in Dell's "Laurel Poetry Series" (1963), which was reprinted the same year in his *Poetry and Fiction: Essays* (Rutgers University Press). Ernest J. Moyne made the most important of all studies of *Hiawatha* in his Hiawatha *and* Kalevala: *A Study of the Relationship Between Longfellow's "Indian Edda" and the Finnish Epic* (Helsinki, Suomalainen Tiedeakatemia Academia Scientiarum Fennica, 1963). In his *Henry Wadsworth Longfellow* (1964), Cecil B. Williams took a fresh look at all Longfellow's writings for "Twayne's United States Authors Series." *The Amazing Mr. Longfellow: Little-Known Facts about a Well-Known Poet*, by Herbert G. Jones (Portland, Maine: The Longfellow Press, 1957) contains some information about Longfellow's haunts. There has also been a somewhat larger number of articles about Longfellow in the learned journals and elsewhere than the general reader might perhaps suppose; relevant items are cited in my notes.

The volume in hand contains the essence of *Longfellow: A Full-Length Portrait*, plus whatever additional materials I have thought it advisable to incorporate. The book has been substantially rewritten, and the plan and organization of the book are quite new. As a biographical portrait, it is, I hope and believe, better balanced and better organized than its predecessor. I renew my thanks to the Longfellow House Trustees for permission to quote from manuscript material and to my friend, Mr. Thomas H. de Valcourt, curator at the Longfellow House, for his continuing assistance. The list of other institutions holding Longfellow materials which I drew upon for *Longfellow: A Full-Length Portrait* appears on p. x of that volume. The publication of the book *American Literary Manuscripts* has now made it much easier to locate scattered letters than when I began my Longfellow studies. I wrote to all the institutions there listed and hereby record my thanks for their courteous replies, for photocopies, microfilms, etc., and, where relevant, for permission to quote.

Readers familiar with *Longfellow: A Full-Length Portrait* will, however, find that there is much less quoted matter in this volume than appeared in its predecessor, and especially that most of the long quotations (complete documents, etc.) have disappeared. When I began my Longfellow work, most of this material had not been printed anywhere, and I thought it important to get it into print and available to scholars, even though in some cases I had to throw my portrait a bit out of balance to get it all in. Since this has now been achieved, there is no need to do it again; there will soon be no dearth of Longfellow documents for anybody. Professor Andrew B. Hilen is editing a complete collection of Longfellow's letters (of which the first two volumes will probably be available about the same time as this book of mine), and Professor Robert Stafford Ward is at work on the journals. I myself have published generous samplings of Mrs. Longfellow's papers in *Mrs. Longfellow: Selected Letters and Journals of Fanny Appleton Longfellow, 1817-1861* (Longmans, Green, 1956). Professor Hilen has been very generous to me during the preparation of this book; it is a pleasure to express my thanks and gratitude here.

EDWARD WAGENKNECHT

West Newton, Mass.
May 14, 1965

CONTENTS

xi

HENRY WADSWORTH LONGFELLOW

BIOGRAPHY

Henry Wadsworth Longfellow was born on February 27, 1807, in Portland, Maine (then a part of the Commonwealth of Massachusetts). He was the second child and son in a family of eight.[1]

The family, which was of Yorkshire yeoman ancestry, had been in America since the middle of the seventeenth century, and its members had devoted themselves to both manual and intellectual pursuits. The poet's father, Stephen Longfellow (1776-1849), was a prominent lawyer and a member of the Hartford Convention who served in both the Massachusetts state legislature and the Congress of the United States.

Through his mother, Zilpah Wadsworth, Longfellow inherited the blood of a number of the Plymouth Pilgrims, including John Alden and Priscilla Mullins, of *The Courtship of Miles Standish*. His maternal grandfather, General Peleg Wadsworth, was a Revolutionary War hero. The boy was named for his uncle, Naval Lieutenant Henry Wadsworth, who died a hero's death in Tripoli harbor in 1804, when he and his companions blew themselves up with the *Intrepid* to save her and themselves from falling into enemy hands.

Henry was a happy, lively, well-behaved little boy, who seems never to have discommoded his parents except as he tended to wear them out with his enthusiastic temperament. He began his education at the age of three at an old-fashioned "dame" school. In 1813 he was sent to the elegantly named Portland Academy, where he studied under Jacob Abbot (later Abbott), the father of Lyman Abbott, and himself destined to fame as the author of the "Rollo" books.

Though Longfellow was an excellent student from the beginning, one cannot but feel that the schools he attended contributed less to his development than the earnest but benevolent atmosphere of his home, where the Puritan highmindedness survived, shorn of all its early harshness and fanaticism, and where both this world and the next were viewed very much in the spirit of William Ellery Channing, who had been a college classmate of Stephen Longfellow's and an important (possibly even determinative) influence upon his religious life.

Stephen Longfellow was a Harvard man, but he sent his two oldest sons together, in 1822, to the new Bowdoin College, at Brunswick, where he was a trustee. Actually, they passed their entrance examinations in 1821, when Henry was fourteen, but they did not take up residence until the beginning of their sophomore year. Henry did as well in college as Stephen did badly and graduated in 1825, in the same class with Nathaniel Hawthorne.

By this time, Longfellow's literary interests were already well established. He had published, serially, both prose and verse, and his future had been made the subject of anxious correspondence between his father and himself. Stephen Longfellow did not fail either to understand or to sympathize with his son's literary ambitions; he simply took his stand on the quite unassailable ground that it would not be safe for the boy to entrust his livelihood to his pen. With his temperament and in his milieu, it was natural that Stephen Longfellow should see the law as the solution of the problem; but to his son, Blackstone's only merit was that he seemed for a time to hold out the hope of a somewhat less harrowing kind of uncongeniality than the horrors of the dissecting room or the terrors of the pulpit.

The young man was not inclined to be either rebellious or unreasonable about the matter. Having secured the generous promise of a year of postgraduate reading in literature at Harvard, he might well have accepted the law had he not been delivered by an inspired Bowdoin trustee, Benjamin Orr, who was so much impressed by his translation of one of Horace's odes that he proposed offering the newly established professorship of modern languages to the young graduate. This proposal was accepted by the Board, on condition that Longfellow should go to Europe at his own expense to fit himself for his new duties.

He sailed from New York on May 15, 1826, and landed, on June 14, at Le Havre. The original purpose of the journey had been to perfect his knowledge of French and Spanish. Before sailing, however, he had a talk with George Ticknor, who urged him by no means to omit Germany, in his view the inevitable center of literary scholarship even in the Romance field. Longfellow's first visit to Europe stretched itself out accordingly to the at first quite uncontemplated length of three years, which he divided between France, Spain, Italy, and Germany. At one point the college reneged on the professorship, offering an instructorship instead, which Longfellow indignantly refused. On August 11, 1829, the young scholar was back in America; on September 6 the Bowdoin trustees voted him his professorship at an annual salary of $800 (the original understanding had been $1000), with an extra $100 for his services as college librarian.

Longfellow taught at Bowdoin from 1829 to 1835. Finding no textbooks which suited him, he made and published his own: *Elements of French Grammar* (1830); *French Exercises* (1830); *Manuel de Proverbes Dramatiques* (1830); *Novelas Españolas* (1830); *Syllabus de la Grammaire Italienne* (1832); *Saggi de' Novellieri Italiani d'Ogno Secolo* (1832). His first poetic publication between covers was his translation of the *Coplas de Jorge Manrique* (1833). His first independent work in prose was the Irving-like *Outre-Mer: A Pilgrimage Beyond the Sea*, published in parts, in imitation of *The Sketch Book*, in 1833 and 1834, and in book form in 1835. This was the only period of his life when Longfellow seemed more interested in scholarship than in creative writing. He contributed a number of learned articles on linguistic and literary subjects to *The North American Review*, and much of this material has not been reprinted.

On September 14, 1831, Longfellow married Mary Storer Potter, daughter of the jurist Barrett Potter, of Portland.

In 1834 Harvard College offered Longfellow the Smith Professorship of French and Spanish which George Ticknor was eager to relinquish. Acceptance would make him, as we should express it today, the "head" of the department of modern languages, imposing responsibility not only for teaching but for organization and supervision as well. And again it was suggested that before taking up his work he should visit Europe for further study.

He sailed from New York in April 1835, with his wife and two of her friends, Clara Crowninshield and Mary Goddard. Miss Goddard was soon recalled to America by the death of her father; Miss Crowninshield remained to the end of the journey, of which her diary has provided a valuable record.[2]

After a brief visit to London, the Longfellow party journeyed to Denmark and Sweden and then to Holland, where Longfellow met the first great sorrow of his life. At Amsterdam, in October, Mary lost the child she had been carrying, and though she rallied afterwards and went on to Rotterdam, she was here taken seriously ill again and died on November 29.

The young widower spent the winter at Heidelberg, attempting to drown his grief in hard study and not succeeding very well. In the spring he went to the Tyrol, whence he intended to proceed to Italy. Passport difficulties intervened and he went to Switzerland instead; this turned out to be one of those curious "accidents" which can change the current of a whole life. For it was here, during the summer of 1836, that Longfellow met those eminently proper Bostonians, Fanny Appleton and her family.

In December 1836 Longfellow arrived in Cambridge. Next summer he established himself in the historic Craigie House, which was to be his home for the rest of his life. At this time it was occupied by the eccentric widow of Andrew Craigie, one-time "apothecary-general" to Washington's army. Being in re-duced circumstances, Mrs. Craigie had been driven to accept lodgers, but her opinion of Harvard students was not a high one, and it cost the young-looking Longfellow some effort to convince her that not only was he a member of the faculty but the author of her much-admired *Outre-Mer*.

Early years in the Craigie House saw the real beginnings of Longfellow's literary career.[3] First, in 1839, came a disorganized, Jean-Paul Richter kind of romance, *Hyperion*, full of German legendry and containing a veiled presentation of his so far un-rewarded love for Fanny Appleton. One of the most important American Romantic documents, *Hyperion* created more stir in its time than posterity finds readily explicable, and European trav-elers used it as a handbook for decades. More permanently sig-nificant was the other 1839 book, the first slim volume of original poems, *Voices of the Night*, some of which, notably "A Psalm of Life," had already, through serial publication, so seized the popular heart and imagination as to make any purely literary evaluation of them even now something of an impertinence.

Two years later, Longfellow published *Ballads and Other Poems* ("The Skeleton in Armor," "The Wreck of the Hesperus," "The Village Blacksmith," "The Rainy Day," "Maidenhood," "Excelsior," etc.). In 1842 he secured leave of absence from his college duties to spend some six months at a water cure in Ger-many, and on his way home, during a stormy passage, he wrote the *Poems on Slavery* (1842), which constituted his contribution to the great moral-political conflict of his time.

In the early summer of 1843 the first stage of Longfellow's life in Cambridge came to a triumphant close with his marriage to Fanny Appleton. He brought her to live at the Craigie House, which was by this time for sale, Mrs. Craigie having died. Shortly afterwards, Nathan Appleton purchased the old mansion with its extensive grounds and presented it to his daughter and her hus-band. Six children were born of this marriage.[4]

In the year of his marriage Longfellow published *The Spanish*

Student, which, though essentially a "closet drama," comes closer to meeting the conditions of theatrical representation than any of his later experiments in the dramatic form.[5] Two years later came *The Belfry of Bruges and Other Poems*, which included, besides the title poem, the equally romantic "Nuremberg"; Mrs. Longfellow's favorite, "The Arsenal at Springfield"; the first important Indian poem, "To a Driving Cloud," and also such popular favorites as "The Bridge," "The Arrow and the Song," and "The Old Clock on the Stairs." In 1847 he published *Evangeline*, his most sustained work to date and the first important long poem in American literature.

Longfellow had not yet, however, committed himself exclusively to the composition of poetry. In 1845 he produced an immense anthology, *The Poets and Poetry of Europe*, containing selections from nearly 400 poets of ten different nationalities, which performed an important service in introducing foreign literature into the United States. He also edited two small collections of fugitive verses: *The Waif* (1845) and *The Estray* (1846). After that he let anthologizing alone until he brought out, in 1876-79, what may well be the most extensive of all poetic anthologies—the thirty-one-volumed *Poems of Places*. Meanwhile he may be said to have taken his leave of prose with *Kavanagh* (1849). This tale of New England village life comes considerably closer to being a novel than does *Hyperion*, but it seems pale and undocumented compared with the work that was coming from Mrs. Stowe, Sarah Orne Jewett, and their successors.

The half-century mark brought the only volume Longfellow devoted entirely to short poems between 1846 and 1867: *The Seaside and the Fireside*. The most important poem was in the "Seaside" section—"The Building of the Ship," that eloquent expression of pre-Civil War hopes which so moved Lincoln. In 1851 Longfellow permitted himself the luxury of an elaborate and somewhat Faustian piece of medievalism, *The Golden Legend*, his most ambitious undertaking to date. It turned out to be caviar to the general, but any ground that he might have lost was more than reclaimed when *The Song of Hiawatha* came out four years later, and in 1858 this was followed by another very successful work, *The Courtship of Miles Standish.*

Except for the resignation of his professorship—a step long pondered, to give him more time to write, but not accomplished until 1854—there had been for many years no "events" in Longfellow's life save the publication of his various books and the birth of his various children. Then, on July 9, 1861, just as the nation was passing under the cloud of civil war, he received the blow which broke his life in two. When Mrs. Longfellow was burned to death, the tragedy ended eighteen years of domestic harmony as perfect as any writer has ever experienced.

Outwardly the change was marked by the alteration in Longfellow's appearance caused by the growth of a full beard, his own burns having made shaving impossible or inadvisable. He found comfort in the care of his children and in his zealous devotion to his translation of *The Divine Comedy* (1867). Before this, however, he had already won another great popular success with the appearance in 1863 of a volume containing the "First Day" of the *Tales of a Wayside Inn* and the "Second Flight" of the lyric poems he called "Birds of Passage." The "First Flight" had already appeared in the same volume with *The Courtship of Miles Standish.*

In 1865 the "Household Edition" of Longfellow's collected poems was issued, and in 1866 came *Flower-de-Luce,* which included his realistic Civil War poem, "Killed at the Ford"; "The Bells of Lynn"; the memorial tribute to Hawthorne; and the first series of sonnets about *The Divine Comedy. The New England Tragedies* followed in 1868; these comprised "John Endicott," which had been written some time before, and "Giles Corey of the Salem Farms." In 1871 came *The Divine Tragedy,* a long-considered semidramatic treatment of the life of Christ. Meanwhile, in 1868-69 he had made his last trip to Europe, where he was lionized. In England Queen Victoria received him in a private audience, and he was given honorary degrees at both Oxford and Cambridge.

Three Books of Song (1872) comprised the "Second Day" of the *Tales of a Wayside Inn;* the brief Apocryphal tragedy, "Judas Maccabeus"; and "A Handful of Translations." In the same year, *The Divine Tragedy, The Golden Legend,* and *The New England Tragedies* were gathered together to form the trilogy, *Christus, A Mystery,* which was designed to explore Christian faith and practice in ancient, medieval, and modern times, though in the last member of the trilogy, which centered upon persecution of witches and Quakers, it was certainly malpractice which occupied the foreground.

The *Tales of a Wayside Inn* was completed in *Aftermath* (1873), which also carried the "Third Flight" of the "Birds of Passage." The most distinguished work in *The Masque of Pandora and Other Poems* (1875) is not in the title piece but in the "Morituri Salutamus," Longfellow's fiftieth-anniversary poem for a Bowdoin College reunion, and a collection of sonnets which, taken with what he had previously produced in this form and what was still to come in the *Kéramos* volume and elsewhere, would give him his high place among English sonneteers. A "Fourth Flight" of the "Birds of Passage" was also included in this volume, as well as his most elaborate celebration of the domestic virtues, "The Hanging of the Crane," which had already been published separately as a lavishly illustrated volume issued during the preceding year.

"Kéramos," the poem about potters and pottery in which Longfellow became something of an imagist before imagism, was handled very much like "The Hanging of the Crane." It, too, first appeared alone, in 1877, then lent its name to *Kéramos and Other Poems* (1878), which also embraced the fifth and last "Flight" of the "Birds of Passage," with more sonnets and translations. Suggestions of foreboding mortality were widely recognized and regretted when *Ultima Thule* appeared in 1880, and Longfellow's instinct was sound, for this was the last of his books that he saw in print. The poems he left uncollected at his death were gathered into *In the Harbor* (1882). In 1882-83 there also appeared the immense fragment, *Michael Angelo,* a dramatic poem which he kept by him during his later years and into which he poured a great deal of his maturest thinking and feeling about art and life, but which he never intended to publish during his lifetime.

Two of Longfellow's children, Ernest and Edith, married before his death, and it was from Edith's children that the old poet derived the greatest pleasure of his later years. His health began to fail rapidly in 1881, and his death, of peritonitis, came after only a few days of illness, on March 24, 1882, less than a month after his seventy-fifth birthday had been celebrated all over America. He was taken sick during the night of March 18-19, but characteristically suffered in silence until morning, though in great pain, not being able to bring himself to disturb his family at an inconvenient hour.

Except for Edgar Allan Poe, who had been dead for more than a generation, he was the first front-ranking American poet of his time to go, and since he was the most famous of them all, his death was widely recognized as marking the beginning of the end of an era.

CHAPTER ONE

"The thoughts of youth are long, long thoughts"

I

Longfellow's contemporaries seem to have found his outer aspect impressive, both in youth and in age. "I do not think," said Charles Kingsley, "I ever saw a finer human face."

A classmate speaks for the college years: "His figure was slight and erect, his complexion light and delicate as a maiden's, with a slight bloom upon the cheek; his nose rather prominent, his eyes clear and blue and his well-formed head covered with a profusion of brown hair waving loosely." Another records his impression when Longfellow returned to Bowdoin as a professor a few years later: "He had a fine, erect figure, a complexion of great purity and delicacy, and a great deal of color. He was youthful in his appearance, and eminently handsome." And when Longfellow came back from Europe in 1842, G. S. Hillard thought him "reduced in flesh perhaps, but a firmer fibre of muscle, and in a better condition of body. His chest seems more expanded, and his complexion more healthy. Were it not for the thick sprinkling of gray among his sunny locks, he might pass for an Apollo, in the glow and prime of his manhood."

When Dickens saw him again after many years, in Boston, in 1867-68, he was struck by his white hair and beard, but still thought him "a remarkably handsome and notable-looking man," "infinitely handsomer," indeed, than when he was younger. In 1871 Mrs. Fields confided to her journal that he had never looked finer. "His white hair and deep blue eyes, and kind face make his presence a benediction wherever he goes." And even when Longfellow was in his seventies, the artist Wyatt Eaton found his vigor noteworthy: "His body seemed forty years younger than his head, never fatigued, always active. . . . Never did I see him walk up the steps leading to the veranda: it was always a skip."

He enhanced his naturally fine appearance by care in dressing. Never, even at home, says his daughter Alice, did he appear "in anything that was at all untidy or unattractive"; neither would he allow others to do so. In youth he was often judged a dandy. In Europe he adopted the fashions of the countries he visited, and when he brought some of these back to America, they were not always appreciated. The reactions of Mrs. Craigie and others in early Cambridge are reflected in *Hyperion*, where the Baron is made to tell Paul Flemming that his gloves are "a shade too light for a strictly virtuous man." The Hasty Pudding Club chronicles of the time contain these verses:

Just twig the Professor dressed out in his best,
Yellow kids and buff gaiters, green breeches, blue vest;
With hat on one whisker and an air that says go it!
Look here! the great North American poet.

There is an amusing letter from Hillard in which he teases Longfellow about a Boston tailor who was so enraptured with the poet's trousers that he wished to borrow them as a model, and Dickens himself (no mean judge in these matters) writes him, after his visit to London, that the boot-maker, the hosier, the trousers-maker, and the coat-cutter "have all been at the point of death" since his departure. "The medical gentlemen agreed that it was exhaustion, occasioned by early rising,—to wait upon you at those unholy hours!" In 1833, when Edward Everett appeared after him at a Phi Beta Kappa meeting at Harvard, he remarked,

"I find myself but a follower in a field where the flashing sickle has already passed." [1]

Longfellow was one of the most frequently limned and, later, photographed men of his time, but this must not be set down to vanity, for, in the years of his celebrity, the initiative was generally taken by others, and he often yielded, even when he would much rather have refused, because it was always difficult for him to turn down any reasonable request. "If I ever sit again to an artist," he exclaims in 1850, "he may make me with asses ears!" But he did not find it possible to keep this brave resolve. Years later, he is still confiding to his journal, "I could not well decline as he was so urgent about it."

When pictures were made, he did not want them to slander him, and he once confessed humorously to Tom Appleton that if he had to choose between good looks and good likenesses, he was all for good looks! In general, however, he seems to have felt that his pictures did not do him justice; once he told his daughter that he wished all his early photographs would fade out. Early in his career he was greatly annoyed by an absurd drawing of himself, which, despite all his efforts to prevent it, appeared in *Graham's Magazine*—"the most atrocious libel imaginable; a very vulgar individual, looking very drunk and very cunning!"

Naturally there have been differences of opinion concerning even the famous likenesses of Longfellow that have come down to us. Personally I quite agree with his brother Alexander about the C. G. Thompson portrait of 1842, which still hangs in the dining room at the Longfellow House: "It has a sneaking, downcast and sinister expression. . . . You look, on that canvas, as if you had been caught stealing sheep, which I am confident you never did." The more attractive portrait by Samuel Lawrence was admired by William Winter because it preserved "that alert, inspired expression which came into his face when he was affected by any strong emotion," but Ernest Longfellow thought it "slightly fierce in expression." "I have just had the pleasure of receiving your photograph," wrote Longfellow to Horatio Bridge in 1875. "It is so good, it could hardly be better. I wish the one I send you in return were as good. But that is wishing I were a handsome man, six feet high, and we all know the vanity of human wishes." This suggests that he was somewhat conscious of his lack of inches: in his Roman journal of 1828 he speaks of himself as a little man, and once at least he suggests a horror of putting on flesh.

Clearly, however, it was not Longfellow's dandyism by which observers were most impressed but his sweet kindliness. Blanche Roosevelt speaks of his eyes as

clear, straightforward, almost proud, yet reassuring. . . . In moments of lofty and inspired speech they have an eagle look, and the orbs deepen and flash. . . . If sad, an infinite tenderness reposes in their depths, and if merry, they sparkle and bubble over with fun. In fact, before the poet speaks, those traitrous eyes have already betrayed his humor.

His voice was another important element in his charm—"those winning accents," as Holmes called them, "too rarely heard in any assembly, and never forgotten by those who listened to them." Elizabeth Peabody told him that he had an *"organ voice* . . . for God not man taught you to read."* And she added: "It is fair that you should do charities with your voice as Jenny Lind with hers." But the most impressive description by far is Bret Harte's:

It was a very deep baritone without a trace of harshness, but veiled and reserved as if he never parted entirely from it, and with the abstraction of a soliloquy even in his most earnest moments. It was not melancholy, yet it suggested one of his own fancies as it fell from his silver-fringed lips

> Like the water's flow
> Under December's snow.[2]

Nothing could better suggest the curiously mingled giving and withholding that was so completely characteristic of Longfellow both as poet and man.

Since it served him for seventy-five years, the body that Long-fellow inhabited must have been a fairly adequate instrument, but he had many illnesses. "Pain never kills any one," he wrote G. W. Greene in 1874, "but is a most uncomfortable bedfellow."

His first serious illness was in childhood, when he suffered an infected foot, which became so bad that at one time amputation was feared. In 1828, while he was living with the Persiani family in Rome, he was very ill with rheumatic fever and might well have died without the devoted nursing of these kindly Italian friends, especially that of the eldest daughter of the house, Mad-ame Julia. During the winter of 1847-48 he was operated upon for a varicose vein. In the summer of 1856 a slight but in its effects persistent injury to his knee compelled him to cancel a proposed trip to Europe. In later years we hear of rheumatism and lumbago and, at the very end, of vertigo and "nervous prostration." During the last year of his life he had a blemish removed from his cheek. The newspapers reported this as a malignant growth; the report annoyed him greatly, and he carefully denied it to all his cor-respondents.

But these comparatively serious disabilities were not what troubled him most. A Bowdoin student in his early teens, he was already seriously concerned about his health. "Ever since I have been here I have been troubled—with a continuing swimming and aching in my head—a fullness and heaviness—I hardly know what to call it. Sometimes a continual pain (at times more or less violent) from morning till night." In 1839 he writes Sam Ward that he has not been well for a year, and by this time he has developed a theory that mental work is the cause. "This *pulling by the head* (as oxen do in some countries) is not conducive to health, I am persuaded." Early in his Harvard professorship, he secures leave to go to Europe for the water cure, whence he sends Sumner a generalization and a dire prophecy, both out-growths of the previously expressed theory. "Begging your par-don for the insult, I do not believe anyone *can* be perfectly well, who has a brain and a heart. *You* will not be well long, and I consider Corny [C. C. Felton] an invalid, though he is not aware of it."

Insomnia plagued him for years. So, too, did "the goddess Neuralgia," who claimed his homage not later than the early 'fifties and never thereafter really let him go; as late as 1876 he complains of an eighteen months' siege. His journals are saturated with neuralgia: it must never be forgotten that he lived much of his life with it as a background. Cold, windy weather always made it worse. "A day of pain; cowering by the fire"—is one entry in 1855. "Great tides of pain go ebbing and flowing among the piers of the teeth perpetually." Besides the neuralgia there was dyspepsia—"almost crazed with this infernal firebrand burning my life out"—which made him feel quite savage at times. These are both demons which moderns know well. But the progress of dental science has largely saved us from the terrible toothaches which afflicted Longfellow. "I am a martyr to toothache; and for three months have not been free from it for a day." In 1838 he had an extraction. "The dentist tugged away merrily . . . for five minutes. At length it came out. He said he never knew one to come so hard." Even so, it did not stop the pain.

But Longfellow had another affliction which, for a writer and scholar, was even worse than these. "Oh for a pair of eyes to work with!"

What was wrong is hard to say. His brother says that shortly before his marriage, he "overstrained his eyes, using them in the twilight," an explanation that I think modern ophthalmologists would regard with considerable skepticism. "Nearly a year ago," he himself writes in June 1844, "writing in the twilight, a partial blindness fell upon me suddenly. For some time I walked in a world of shadows, seeing men as trees. By great care (and no coffee) I have now got so far as to write a short letter, and to read at intervals during the day, an hour or two in all."

In the first year of their marriage, he and Fanny went to New York to consult the great Dr. Samuel Elliott, who was as reassuring as he could be. But progress was slow. "I still remain half blind," he writes in 1848, "seeing only at favorable hours and in favorable lights." In these years, Mrs. Longfellow, fortunately herself an excellent linguist, was both able and willing to lend him her eyes. It is hard to see how he could have done his work without her. Because of his handicap, he scrawled the first draft of *Evangeline* before the fire, without looking at his pad.

Longfellow was never fanatical about medical theory—as late as 1867 he had his whole family vaccinated—but insofar as he had any convictions in this area, he was a homeopath. He urged homeopathy upon his father as early as 1841, and it troubled him to have his son Charley treated by allopath after he had been wounded in the Civil War. He also had an unshaken faith in hydropathy, to which he submitted himself both in Europe and in America, and which he urged tirelessly upon his friends. Fanny found it difficult to believe that a summer at Brattleboro would help his eyes, "but," she says, "I think his general health will undoubtedly [benefit]; he enjoys the perpetual bathing so much, and is tempted with so much exercise and appetite." He himself was unshaken, even when the results were less impressive than he had expected. "If I could have staid through the Autumn, I should have come back in the first order, with a new pair of eyes and stomach to match." Once he even recommended the water cure to his brother Stephen as a remedy for loss of memory!

But he did not confine himself to hydropathy or to any one remedy. Once he devoted himself to early rising, an egg in milk, and a short walk in the shade. For insomnia he ranged all the way from sleeping medicines to willing himself to sleep, but the cure for neuralgia in the shape of a medicated belt and breastplate brought by a "mysterious stranger" was the most picturesque thing he essayed. He even sent this to his great friend, George Washington Greene, but that man of many ills derived no benefit from it whatever. Longfellow was as experimental about it as Sir Francis Bacon himself could have desired. "Perhaps you did not wear it long enough," he wrote. "Perhaps there is no virtue in it." And he added, "I have had a very hard week of it. The headache continues unabated and sometimes worse than ever. Nothing does it any good except the mild weather."

From many forms of allegedly healthful exercise Longfellow was almost automatically debarred by his indifference to sport. His sister Annie denies that this went back to his boyhood: "I should say he was fond of all boys' games, balls, kites, swimming, and snowballing, coasting, and skating." But she adds: "He was too tender hearted to enjoy gunning and shooting birds with his brother. I well remember his coming home one day with his eyes full of tears, and *so* grieved in heart because he had shot a robin." Henry's early horror of guns was one of the things his mother told Fanny about on her first visit to Portland, and Fanny was pleased to find that he shared this trait with her. In later years, when his daughter Edith visited the White Mountains, she found it unnatural to think of her father as having enjoyed the so-called "manly" sports there, even in his youth. She writes with gentle irony, "Then as we passed through Hiram we saw the old Wadsworth house in the distance through the trees, and Rattlesnake mountain where as tradition says the Poet Longfellow used to play in his youthful days—a sort of infant Hercules I suppose."

Frank Stearns says that Longfellow persuaded his son Charley to give up pigeons for target shooting, and even objected to the shooting of crows until it was explained to him that they preyed on songbirds. Once he thanks a correspondent for a poem about fox-hunting, "beautiful notwithstanding its subject, for which I have no sympathy." In 1858-59 he was tempted to join an "Adirondack Club," but finally decided against it:

Agassiz, Lowell, Emerson and some others have gone to the Adirondack country, to camp out and do many wonders. Agassiz is to weigh the brains of trout, which the others are to catch. Emerson has bought himself a double-barreled shot gun for the occasion; on hearing which, I respectfully declined joining the party! They have been out ten days, and so far we have not heard of anybody's being shot.[3]

Longfellow's "views" on the subject of exercise ranged all the way from his early notion that his frame required a great deal of it to his late, probably humorous, remark to Howells that putting on his overcoat and overshoes was quite enough. From time to time he went in for walking, skating, rowing, boxing, swimming, gardening, and using an apparatus in the house, but he does not seem to have been zealous or consistent with any of these. Even walking had its drawbacks. "But I begin to find that it takes two to take a walk; yes, and a *dog*." It is clear that bathing was what he enjoyed most—"my element is cold water"—and there is one rapturous description of "a magnificent bath" at evening in the river, "the sunset seeming to mingle with the water." But by the time Richard Henry Dana became his son-in-law not even this tempted him greatly; neither did he care for sailing; in fact, he always had the idea that he did not feel well during his summers at Nahant.

In these days of "psychosomatic" medicine, one can hardly avoid asking whether there was an element of hypochondria in Longfellow's illnesses. The question arises again in connection with his brother Sam, whose "poor health" is blamed for his having had a much less important ministerial career than his undoubted abilities would seem to have qualified him for. Both Longfellow's father and his mother were invalids during their later years.

Longfellow more than once calls himself a hypochondriac, though perhaps this is the best proof we could ask that he was not one really. "The heart of a hypochondriac is like a chamber, into which the sun never shines; and whose windows look out on a graveyard. All within is sad and sombre; all without reminds him of the end of his nature." "A kind of sleepiness of the soul," he calls it once, "in which I feel a general indifference to all things." When Sam Ward was ill, he advised him to seek "the seat and origin" of his complaint "in the heart and not in the stomach." And after he had hurt his knee in 1856 Mrs. Longfellow suggested to Sumner that the injury was not wholly physical. "I think he would be refreshed if once in Europe, but he has no heart to go."

If Longfellow was a hypochondriac, it is clear that he was a singularly patient one. "You must not . . . be troubled about me," he writes as late as 1875. "I shall worry through it." Despite all his ills, he was fortunate in being able to retain much of his physical vigor and nearly all his mental vigor well into old age. It is true that he seemed much older after Fanny died, but this was simply because so much of his joy in life had gone with her. He was not unmindful of either the passing years or the terror of mortality. As he approaches his fifty-eighth birthday, he finds that "anniversaries are growing too sad to talk about. The milestones begin to look like tombstones, and one seems to be whirling along through a churchyard." Nor does he wonder that Greene should shrink from preparing George Sumner's reminiscences. "Old letters are very sad and depressing. I have a good mind to burn all I have. I certainly shall never read them." Yet he clung to the past and was apparently quite incapable of burning anything.

In the larger aspects, however, nobody ever grew old more gracefully. It is only in little things that the strain shows, as in his rebuke to Ticknor, who tried to help him on with his overcoat: "Never do that. A young man does not need it, and an old man does not want it." Once the conductor of a public vehicle cried out loudly upon his entrance, "Please pass forward and make room for this old gentleman." "I consoled myself," says Longfellow, "as well as I could with the remembrance that even the Roman Emperors in their triumphs had some one to remind them that they were mortal."

III

Probably no man ever achieved eminence with less strenuousness in his disposition than Longfellow. *Non clamor, sed amor* was the quite characteristic motto on his bookplate, and Wordsworth himself was not more sure that

The gods approve
The depth, and not the tumult of the soul.

"He did not flare out in convulsive eruptions," writes James Taft Hatfield, "but fulfilled his missions *ohne Hast, aber ohne Rast.*"

One visitor reports his closing all the shutters of his house against a thunderstorm and remarking that he disliked anything violent. He found it difficult to believe in the necessity of painful or strenuous methods even in medicine, and when he read Frémont's account of his Rocky Mountain expedition, the hardships impressed him more than the adventure. Before the Civil War at least, all that kind of thing seemed to belong largely to the past: "At the present day we are seldom called upon for the exercise of heroic virtue."

Even in his dealings with books this comforting note is struck. Sumner, he tells Greene in 1877, "brought away from Italy a vast amount of knowledge; while I brought away little more than memories and impressions,—a kind of golden atmosphere, which has always illuminated my life." Sumner's zest in reading amazed him too, and his insatiability in such matters as looking at pictures. "For my part," says Longfellow, "I cannot take in so much at once. It fatigues my brain and body." Though he had a scholar's appreciation of great tragedy, his sensitiveness often made it impossible for him to enjoy it. In 1860 Fanny Kemble's reading of *Othello* put him out of spirits all next day, and the next night he stayed away from *Hamlet*, though it was the last evening of Mrs. Kemble's season, and he was devoted to her. He was glad, too, when he got through with translating the "Inferno" portion of *The Divine Comedy*, and the reading of *The Greek Anthology* inspired melancholy. Like his own Ser Federigo, he always tended to believe that

"All things come round to him who will but wait,"

or, as Ernest Longfellow puts it,

... he always thought it best not to do a thing. He had none of the adventurous spirit. "To stay at home is best," he wrote. He hated excess or extremes. He disliked extreme cold or extreme heat, and believed in the *juste milieu* in everything.... He was not a rushing river, boiling and tumbling over rocks, but the placid stream flowing through the quiet meadows.

One would expect such a man to be very sensitive to his surroundings. In *Hyperion* Longfellow remarks that "there are persons in this world to whom all local associations are naught. The genius of the place speaks not to them." There was never a man to whom "the genius of the place" spoke more eloquently than to him; this is why he was so eminently fitted for the editorship of *Poems of Places*. But even when he found himself where he most loved to be, a shadow across the face of the sun could spoil everything. "My mornings are glorious, and so are the evenings and nights. But the afternoons, the last three hours of the sun, are inexpressibly gloomy." Even his lectures were spoiled for him if he had to give them in an unsuitable room or before unattractive listeners. "How very sensitive I am to the appearance of my scholars."

He was the child of a beautiful city and a pleasant, comfortable home. The Wadsworth-Longfellow House was two years a-building, the first house in Portland whose all four walls were brick. The brick was brought from Philadelphia, and there was enough of it to make the walls sixteen inches thick. The parlor, largest in the city, had the first piano in the area.

When the young man went to college at Brunswick, he found it necessary to live under very Spartan conditions, but even then he called upon his sisters to decorate his rooms for him. When he went abroad the first time, he tried to live as economically as possible, yet "respectably and genteelly." The first house he occupied after his marriage pleased him except for "the style of the paper-hangings, which cry aloud against the taste of my landlord and predecessor." There were stripes, and there were parrots, and he could endure neither. At the Craigie House, on the other hand, he had beautiful surroundings from the beginning, and as fame and wealth came, with the house in his own possession, he crammed it with *objets d'art* and thousands upon thousands of books, creating a scholar's paradise which has happily been preserved to delight the scholars of a later day. His "playthings," as he called them, included the land and the view as well as the house, for in his time Craigie House was a country residence.

Ernest Longfellow speaks of the satisfaction the poet always found in the view of the Charles from his front door: "often have I seen him come out on his front steps bareheaded, merely to gaze at it, either in its noonday haze or lit up with the splendors of sunset." Nor did he ever spare effort to keep everything just the way he wanted it. Nobody who has visited Emerson's house at Concord, Massachusetts, will need to be told that the sage did not live in squalor there, yet he seems to have been repelled by the sybaritism he sensed in Cambridge: "If Socrates were here, we could go and talk with him; but Longfellow we cannot go and talk with; there is a palace, and servants, and a row of bottles of different colored wines, and wine glasses, and fine coats."

At Nahant it was all very different, but Longfellow was never really happy at Nahant, though he continued to spend his summers there because the family loved the place. "For a vacation life, it is altogether too still and uneventful. We have quiet enough and solitude in Cambridge. For a change we need more society and more gaiety." Moreover he was "cooped up in a small house, in the village, with only a strip of sea in sight," and "without a table to write on" or "hardly a place to lay a book." Fanny understood and sympathized with these difficulties, but she was also intelligent enough not to take them too seriously. Once he wanted to shift his summers to Stockbridge, "and if I did not remember his sufferings from heat at the Melville House," says Fanny, looking back to the time they had stayed there, "I should think it probably best for all of us—but the children thrive here, certainly, famously," and so she decided to stay at Nahant, knowing in her heart that he would be no better off inland, once the novelty had worn off.

One thing was certain: inland or on the seashore, there was no controlling the weather. Once Longfellow declared that he did not "care a fig for the weather, if I can only be left quiet," but this was a curiously uninformed self-judgment. He was much more accurate when he wrote: "The weather is cruel; and I who depend so much upon climate for pleasant sensations, suffer martyrdom."

Apparently he suffered more actual discomfort from cold than many people do. "Bitter cold; six degrees below zero. What a foe to civilization such cold weather is! Who wants to shave, or dress, or be elegant in such weather!" For him this was indeed sounding the depths.

Fog struck Longfellow as romantic—"mysterious, transfiguring all things"—but he often expresses his dislike for what other people regard as the much more romantic snow. "The first snow is beautiful. The pure and spotless flakes descend to the earth like the souls of children." But when it blanketed the earth and swallowed up everything else and blotted it out, he was oppressed and overwhelmed by it, as Katherine Mansfield was. Once he even notes that it produces nausea, "particularly when melting in the sun," and attributes this to its effect on the nerves of the eye. So what he really liked was "a snowless winter," with "brown, bare branches against purple skies morning and evening."

But it was not only bad weather which lowered Longfellow's resistance, and wore him out, and made him incapable of producing anything; good weather often had the same effect. Sometimes inspiration was lacking, sometimes leisure, sometimes merely the will. Intellectually he may have been "convinced that it is sheer laziness, when a poet refrains from writing because he is 'not in the mood,'" etc., but the excuse appears in his journals again and again. "The lazy days drag onward. I cannot write." "Cannot get back into the poetic mood." And, more elaborately: "Truly I know not how the days pass. A letter, a lecture—and lo! it is dinner time! A walk in the garden and lo! it is evening. A sleep, a forgetfulness—and lo! it is morning!"

Like Milton, he always expected a revival of poetic power with the autumn—perhaps this is why October was his favorite month—but it did not always come. Nor was it only in summer that his sluggishness plagued him. Once he records, amusingly, having attended a lecture at which there were "only eleven people, and four of them asleep, of which I was one." And it was in March that he repined over the bitter necessity of creeping to bed at nine because he could not stay awake, "stuffed with daylight, like a drowsy peasant 'stuffed with distressful bread.'" His principal complaint against teaching was that it kept him from writing, yet he often wasted the leisure he had, and after he had retired he showed a tendency to transfer the blame for the lack of productiveness he still lamented to the demands of social and family life.

In his youth Longfellow was an eager traveler who bravely turned his dreams of absorbing Old World culture into reality, and during his early years in Cambridge, when academic duties kept him at home, he was eager to return to Europe: "I chanced to cast my eye this morning upon a map of Italy, where my old route was marked in red,—the red vein of my young life-blood. Instantly I went mad for travel. It is spring, and the sun shines bright; and it seems a waste of life to stay here." But after his retirement, when he could have gone any time he chose, he went only once, in 1868, for by this time he preferred to do his traveling in books; indeed, packing to get ready to go to Nahant disturbed him almost as much as packing up for Europe. "I wish that you would come here for once," Bernard Roelker wrote him from New York. "I should like to go with you to my favorite spots in Central Park. But you seem to have become stationary, and live in your accustomed place without change." Charles Sumner was much hurt in 1868, when Longfellow would not visit him in Washington before sailing, and expressed his disappointment pathetically, but Longfellow was unmoved. "I wish you were going to Europe instead of me," he replied; "for I had rather stay at home." In July he wrote Sumner from Shanklin, "Travelling is a Paradise of Fools! as someone has said before," and though there is other evidence to show that he enjoyed the journey more than he had expected to enjoy it, he did not change his attitude at all. "I have just met Horsford in the street," he wrote Greene in 1880. "He is going to Europe with one or two of his daughters! How glad I am that I am not going!"

Moreover, there were times when Longfellow's apathy passed over into a positive, active misery. "Misericordia! I have fallen into a state of dullness and apathy quite woeful! No life—no keen sensations; but a dismal lethargy hanging about me like a darkness." Those who met Longfellow got little or no inkling of this side of his nature, and I am sure he did not inflict it upon those he lived with. Probably it seldom got beyond a journal entry, and even here he was restrained by his knowledge that "death picks the locks of all portfolios, and throws the contents into the street for the public to scramble for." Samuel Longfellow carefully edited most of this material out of the journal entries he printed, but plenty of it remains in the manuscript; it is about the only thing that makes the journals, at times, dull reading. Sometimes it even goes to the length of a mystical terror and foreboding. "O heavy heart, be comforted! A kind of panic and wild alarm has seized upon me, which I cannot control! God be merciful to me!" And, a few months later: "I have fallen into a strange state of discouragement and apathy of mind. It seems as if some great change—some great destiny were impending over me. I am restless, and my imagination is filled with images of gloom." Not even his completely happy marriage seems to have been able to produce abiding good spirits in him.

The odd thing about Longfellow's temperament is that this lethargy should have co-existed with so many other qualities not ordinarily associated with it. He certainly was not considered melancholy as a child. "An active rogue," his mother calls him at two, "wishes for nothing but singing and dancing." He was a "bright, pleasant boy" also, "sensitive, impressionable; active, eager, impetuous, often impatient; quick-tempered, but as quickly appeased; kind-hearted and affectionate,—the sun-light of the house." After he had left for Europe, his mother wrote, "I will not say how much we miss your elastic step, your cheerful voice, your melodious flute."

He retained much of this when he grew older; indeed he retained a feeling of youth into mature years. "His coming into our house," said one of the intimates of the Bowdoin years, "was always like sunshine." And when George Washington Greene invited him, as an old man, to his daughter's wedding, he said, "Half the sunshine will be taken away if you are not here." Certainly Longfellow always thought of himself as possessing an

ardent and enthusiastic nature—"such an ardent nature as mine";
"my rather effervescent nature"—so much so indeed that he sometimes considered drudgery itself a useful ballast.

> Through every fibre of my brain,
> Through every nerve, through every vein,
> I feel the electric thrill, the touch,
> Of life, that seems almost too much.

There could hardly be a more generous and romantic temperament than that which Longfellow attributed to his other self,
Paul Flemming, in *Hyperion*, and he nearly matches Paul in his
early letters to his father about his future literary career.

He himself said, "I am at one and the same time listless and
restless." [4] It may be that the lethargy was physical and the ardor
temperamental, or it may be that the mixture was more compli-
cated than that. One thing is certain: there was a good deal of
tension in Longfellow's inner being, and the understanding description of "nerves" which he achieved in "The Beleaguered
City" and "The Haunted Chamber" was not based on imagination
alone.

> What are ye, O pallid phantoms!
> That haunt my troubled brain?
> That vanish when day approaches,
> And at night return again? [5]

Some conflicts, some areas of experience a man of such sensitiveness must learn to ignore—unless he wishes to kill himself. There
are times when Longfellow comes close to attributing sensitiveness
to inanimate objects, as when, noting the arrival of a steamer, he
adds, "What a night she must have had of last night—with the
snow and the wind." He could be almost smug about the "painful
tone" of Hawthorne's books, "deeper even than a minor key, . . .
as if written by a fallen angel," yet his Inaugural Address at Bowdoin found melancholy in the nature of the poetic temperament
itself. But the element of self-control was always there, and though
he was not too thick-skinned to know self-doubt, he never allowed
it to overwhelm him. And so he writes, at one stage, even about

Evangeline: "As I read, I grow discouraged. Alas, how difficult it is to produce anything really good! Now I see nothing but the defects of my work. I hope the critics will not find as many as I do. But onward! The poem, like love, must 'advance or die.' "

It did advance, and so did his work in general, and his living also. It was in this spirit that he met his long disappointment during his wooing of Fanny Appleton, and however trite "A Psalm of Life" may seem to us, it did mark a genuine crisis in his own spiritual experience and a resolute turning away from what he had come to regard as the instability of his earlier career.[6] He thought of this as a braver and a more sensible, more Christian way of meeting his difficulties than that exemplified by Werther, and in this he was quite right. Moreover, he published his spiritual autobiography, *Hyperion*, well knowing the criticism it would evoke, but no less determined, therefore, to express what was in him. I do not see how the publication of that work can be defended in this aspect as an act of either good taste or good judgment, but it was certainly an act of courage.

Longfellow's humor was also useful to him in this connection, and he had more humor than those who know him only by his poetry are aware. As Ernest remarks, he "was fond of making harmless puns and small witticisms." These are found scattered through his letters and journals, and most of them are not very good. He had the habit, too, of recording idle chitchat and amusing encounters, most of which seem to have pleased him more than they have pleased many readers, though we certainly could not have spared his account of the three belated Boston ladies who trailed down the aisle to their front seats at Fanny Kemble's reading of *Macbeth*, just as the actress was intoning

> What are these,
> So withered and so wild in their attire
> That look not like th' inhabitants of the earth,
> And yet are on't?

Indeed, verbal humor of every kind amused him, whether it took the form of the malapropism of the Pole who was charmed by the lady's "dotage" (meaning "dowry") or was produced by the heavy accent of the German woman who called "The Building of the Ship" "The Lunch of the Sheep." Though he seems to have relished Lowell's labored humor in desiring to apply to scholars who tampered unnecessarily with Shakespeare's text "the quadri-syllabic name of the brother of Agis, king of Sparta" (Euda-midas), I think he was never guilty of anything so ponderous upon his own account, though I admit his apostrophe to winter, upon returning, as "for his umbrella," on February 18, 1838, is not wonderfully spontaneous: "Begone, old man, and wag not thy hoary beard at me!"

Longfellow was fond, too, of curiosa of every innocent descrip-tion, and often clipped startling or ridiculous "personals" from the newspapers and sent them to his friends. One letter to Sumner contains a number of such clippings, of which this is the most startling:

MATRIMONIAL. Will some fair one correspond with me? I am 28 years of age, am pretty good looking, dark curly hair, dark eyes, height 5 ft. 10 in., straight as an arrow, generous to a fault, love sport, have a keen perception of the ridiculous, and can love, oh! *how* I can love! Just try me. Address HENRY P. HARTFORD, Boston.

And in 1872 he sent this clipping to Greene:

DON'T HOPE

To escape me by leaving Paris with your wife. Every movement shall be watched. I have not found you to lose you. From me there is no escape.   "Cora" at termination of Act 2d, in "Article 47."

But Longfellow's humor did not stop on this primitive level, and if it had it could not have served him very notably as spiritual ballast. He had that capacity for detached observation of himself and his concerns which is the true mark of the comic spirit. In 1840 fire destroyed the outbuildings at the Craigie House. "Had there been a West wind," he writes his father, "the spot where I sit writing, would now be some twenty feet up in the open air, without roof or floor." Though he seems not to have liked his name, he was delighted by the little girl who, finding a daddy longlegs crawling over her pillow, cried out that Mr. Longfellow was in her room. He once offered to read Greene his latest poem as a cure for sleeplessness, and it is he who preserves the record of the Englishman who came to see him because there were no ruins in America, to say nothing of the Irishman who was delighted to meet a poet because he had a brother who was a poet—and, he added, "a drunkard." Even the terrible Count Gurowski, that monstrous consumer of time, is made to yield such amusement as he can. "We feel," records the poet after one visit, "as if a huge garden-roller had gone over us." When his face is swollen with the toothache he reminds himself of Henry VIII, and when his head throbs he feels a sewing machine inside, "turning out any amount of ready-made clothing." Even after Fanny Appleton has apparently turned him down, he can speak of his late serious accident in Beacon Street.[7]

This was useful as comic relief, but the real solution of Longfellow's emotional problems had to be sought at a deeper level. The very tendencies I have already noted as making for sluggishness and lethargy appear in a more attractive and positive aspect in the calmness and serenity of spirit which his friends never failed to sense during his lifetime and which appears so prominently in his poetry. "Paul Revere's Ride," for example, is primarily an action-piece, and as such it is splendidly successful, but I am sure that every sensitive reader of Longfellow must feel that the poet strikes his most characteristic note in the interlude in which the hero's friend, having climbed to "the tower of the Old North Church," pauses

> to listen and look down
> A moment on the roofs of the town,
> And the moonlight flowing over all.

Ruskin felt this steadying, calming effect of Longfellow's presence very strongly, and Whittier, implicationally, and therefore all the more convincingly, testifies to the same quality when, having read *Evangeline*, he rejoices that he himself did not write about the expulsion of the Acadians as he had once intended to do. "If I had attempted it I should have spoiled the artistic effect of the poem by my indignation at the treatment of the exiles by the Colonial government."

"Let us die standing." So Longfellow writes Sumner, as he waits for the carriage to come and take him to Hawthorne's funeral. And he adds, "I am full of faith, hope, and good heart!" That this spirit survived into old age, a great passage in "Morituri Salutamus" remains to testify; it never failed him for long.

> All thought and feeling and desire, I said,
>   Love, laughter, and the exultant joy of song
>   Have ebbed from me forever! Suddenly o'er me
> They swept again from their deep ocean bed,
>   And in a tumult of delight, and strong
>   As youth, and beautiful as youth, upbore me.

There is a spiritual quality about this achieved serenity of Longfellow's which must not be attributed altogether to nature. It did not "come" spontaneously; there was an element of spiritual discipline and self-conquest involved; and it is not fair to him to ignore the seething world of "nerves" and passion that lay beneath his seeming placidity. Horace E. Scudder was quite right when he declared that "there was no mere avoidance of disturbing elements, nor was his serenity the result of favoring conditions; his nature asserted itself in a resolute composition of conditions. ... He deliberately chose and refrained according to a law in his members, and took clear cognizance of his nature and its tendencies."

CHAPTER TWO

"The ideal and the actual in our life"

I

Like other men, Longfellow had to live with others as well as himself, and it is not without significance that one must begin here with the negative aspect.

Even in his college days, one of his classmates speaks of him as "rather disinclined to general intercourse," adding that "it appeared easy for him to avoid the unworthy." As a professor at Bowdoin, he disclaimed interest in a large circle of acquaints. "I like intimate footings; I do not care for general society." He always rejoiced that the New York custom of paying New Year's calls did not prevail in Boston, for he could see no point in "speeding from house to house, from morning to night, through mud and rain, snow, or sleet, merely to gratify hundreds of people, who expect you to enact this folly."

In Cambridge, too, he was sometimes considered aloof; as Howells remarks, he was more detached from the local scene than his friends and neighbors; "he was Longfellow to the friends who were James and Charles and Wendell to one another." "I came to know Longfellow on the street," writes Nathaniel S. Shaler, "and had many pleasant exchanges with him in our meetings; he would sometimes turn and walk with me, or bid me go

33

with him. We often met at the houses of mutual friends, but he never bade me to his own." His son-in-law, Richard Henry Dana, doubted that there was anyone except his wife, "and possibly Felton," with whom he really cast off reserve. "In his eye, which looked at you so frankly and squarely and with such tenderness, there was an alarm on the first turn of the conversation to anything personal to himself." Alice Longfellow admits this reserve also, though she insists that it was "not caused by any self absorption, or lack of interest in others, but on the contrary, by an extreme delicacy of feeling that made it impossible for him to touch upon subjects very close to himself, or to run the risk of touching the inner life of another in even the most tender manner." Longfellow himself declares that "with me, all deep impressions are silent ones. I like to live on, and enjoy them, without telling those around me that I do enjoy them." And there is the delightful story of the friend who, disappointed at his failure to elicit certain information from the poet, said, "Yet you confessed to me once." "No," replied Longfellow, with a laugh, "I think I never did."

None of this means, however, that he was a hermit, or that he desired to be. Fanny, indeed, thought him "especially social by nature." Certainly he placed no exaggerated value upon either privacy or solitude. He is sure that it does Washington Allston no good to live so much alone. "Rust seems gathering on his mind." Nor should the scholar or writer withdraw into a corner. If he would describe the world, he must live in the world.

After Fanny's death, Longfellow's interest in society fell off sharply, and during his later years he was notably disinclined toward going anywhere. "It will give me great pleasure to promise to come," he once wrote Fields, "with the understanding that you do not expect me to keep my promise." But during his early years in Cambridge this was not at all the case. Before his second marriage, when he first came to Harvard, he found himself quite the society man. "There is such a social spirit here and in Boston, that I seldom see a book by candlelight. Indeed, I pass half my evenings, at least, in society—it being almost impossible to avoid it."

Afterwards there was a reasonable attendance upon formal entertainments, balls, etc., where Longfellow's principal source of
enjoyment was always the admiring contemplation of his wife's
beauty in her formal dress; but they both cared much more for
informal entertainments at home, and here, it would seem, the
latch-string was always out.

No man was less of a snob than Longfellow. "But often," says
Howells, "the man who dined with Longfellow was the man who
needed a dinner; and from what I have seen of the sweet courtesy
that governed that board, I am sure that such a man could never
have felt himself the least honored guest." Dana speaks of his
going to the door on one occasion to call to a stranger who was
gazing at the house and invite him in. But though he did not
confine himself to exclusive circles, they were always open to
him, both at home and abroad. This is not surprising so far as
the later years are concerned, when he had become an institution,
and nearly every distinguished visitor to Boston, from royalty
on down, found the way to his door. But it does seem surprising
that the unknown Portland boy who went to Europe at nineteen,
with letters of introduction to various distinguished men who had
never heard of him before, should have been received so unquestioningly. Lafayette sent greetings and tickets to the Chamber of
Deputies as soon as he heard of his arrival in Paris, and only
Bulwer-Lytton seems to have snubbed him.[1]

Though Longfellow could "scintillate" on occasion, generally
speaking he was neither a gifted conversationalist nor a brilliant
host. On this point the testimony of his intimates coincides with
that of those who only met him casually. Thus his son Ernest
speaks of "a memorable lunch at Nahant," attended by Holmes,
Sumner, Agassiz, Tom Appleton, and Longfellow. "It would be
hard," he says, "to find four more wonderful talkers than the first
four." Ruskin calls Longfellow "a quiet and simple gentleman,
neither especially frank nor reserved, somewhat grave, very pleasant, not amusing, strangely innocent and calm, caring little for
things out of his serene sphere." "He did not talk much himself,"
says Howells, "and I recall nothing that he said. But he always

spoke both wisely and simply, without the least touch of pose, and with no intention of effect, but with something that I must call quality for want of a better word." When he stopped coming to the Saturday Club after Fanny's death, Hawthorne thought the dinner table deprived of much of its charm, "for though he was not brilliant, and never said anything that seemed particularly worth hearing, he was so genial that every guest felt his heart the lighter and the warmer for him." In short, it seems to have been very much with the man as it is with the poet: the effect which he creates is hardly to be accounted for by the enumeration of his specific gifts and powers.[2]

Judged by our (obviously quite irrelevant) modern standards, Longfellow's social intercourse often seems somewhat formal. It seems that even the children were sometimes conscious of this. Both Ernest and Alice found Sumner what might now be called "stuffy," though Annie Allegra loved him, and recorded her affection in a manuscript called "A Little Person's Memories of Great People." [3]

During his later years, Longfellow's social life inevitably surrounded itself with a certain atmosphere of adulation, and we get some pictures of his holding forth rather tritely to a beatific company of adoring disciples. But allowance must always be made in these cases for the *Schwärmerei* or sycophantism of the reporter, as notably with Blanche Roosevelt. Longfellow came through the ordeal as unspoiled as any man could have been expected to do so, though if Madame Roosevelt is right about his extreme sensitiveness in old age, this must have acted as a kind of damper upon social ease and freedom:

Without saying anything, one could see at once that some antagonistic element had forced its presence upon him, and he received at the same moment an instantaneous shock. He shivers mentally, and reminds one of a sensitive plant that, taken from its natural surroundings, is transplanted to the wayside, and feels for the first time the chill, piercing blast, and cold discomfort of an uncongenial clime. I sometimes think so impressionable a nature a doubtful gift.

Persons less "impressionable" than "the American Aurora" herself seem to have felt this also, as, for example, the artist Wyatt Eaton, who felt a sense of constraint when he came to paint Longfellow that he had not felt at all with Emerson and others. For one thing, he did not dare remove his coat, though the day was very warm, and, as the hours passed, he found good reason to rejoice that he had not so ventured. For when a visitor brought the astonishing tidings that in Boston offices were men who were beginning to remove their coats in summertime, the poet seemed to be shocked. "At least they might have some kind of light jacket to put on, to have the appearance of a coat." Yet he could be surprisingly liberal about larger things. He tolerated outrageous gaucherie from Joaquin Miller, nor does he seem to have been repelled by Oscar Wilde's idiosyncrasies and affectations, when the latter called upon him in 1882.

Nor did Longfellow wholly eschew the indulgences which many people seem to think indispensable to social life. The cellar at the Craigie House was well stocked with fine wines, which were regarded as an important part of the dinners served there. Longfellow gave and received numerous gifts of wine, and sometimes ordered it in large quantities; once he even offered champagne, along with cigars and coffee, to an Arabian guest! It is true that once or twice in his life he gave up drinking wine, but this seems to have been purely a dietary measure. When he attended a dinner at which no wine was served, it always seemed to him a poor thing. On the other hand, Alice Longfellow insists that her father did not approve of hard liquors, and there are very few references to these among his memorabilia. Once he tried whiskey to cure neuralgia, but this was simply a phase of his never-ending experimentation in the search for remedies; he would probably have tried arsenic if anybody had suggested it to him.

About the only suggestion of over-stimulation occurs in Clara Crowninshield's European journal of 1838, where she records his having returned home from a function where he had tasted twenty different wines. "His face was flushed," she says, "and our laughing at him, or really the effects of the wine, confused him so

much that he could not count the money straight to pay the bill."
Hoffmann's drinking is censured in *Hyperion*, and the paper on
Anglo-Saxon literature sees mankind "reeling through the Dark
Ages." Thomas Campbell's brandy drinking was one of the aspects of his "outward man" which disappointed Longfellow when
they met in 1843, though he "liked his inward man exceedingly."
He was shocked by the Spanish fountain which was made to spout
wine upon a festival occasion, shocked by the drinking, smoking,
and card-playing of the Swedish clergy, and shocked by a celebration in honor of "the Swedish Anacreon," Carl Michael Bell-
man, whose bust showed him "leering from his pedestal, with
bloated cheeks and sleepy eyes, as if awaking from last night's
debauch. Out upon the young men of Stockholm for honoring
the memory of such a man in this way!" "The Ladder of St.
Augustine" classifies "the revel of the ruddy wine" with more
serious "occasions of excess"; Michael Angelo loves not wine and
avoids the banquet where it is to be served; and "The Revel of
Earl Sigvald," which was finally excluded from "The Saga of
King Olaf," contains these lines:

> Feasts kill more than fighting;
> Drinking more than smiting;
> Swords are sharp, but sharper
> Is the Drinking Horn!

In Longfellow's projected Robin Goodfellow play, alcoholic bev-
erages were to appear among the curses that afflict mankind. He
approved of the Maine liquor law, being unable to go along with
his friend Scherb's displeasure over the prospect of "banishing
young Bacchus, and all the poetry of vintages." On the other
hand, when it was proposed to subject Harvard professors to the
same regulations concerning drinking as those by which the students were governed, he rebelled. But this was not a clear case,
for drinking, theater, and opera had all been idiotically jumbled
together.

Longfellow was no slave to the pleasures of the table either,
though judged by modern standards, the board at the Craigie

House would seem lavish. Of one dinner for the Lowells, Fredrika Bremer, and Charlotte Cushman he records, "We fed them canvasback ducks, quails, Roman punch, and three kinds of American wines, Sparkling Catawba, Cabella, and Scuppernong." Yet the most ecstatic food passage in his journals sings the praises of bread and butter, and Alice Longfellow says that as her father grew older, he "cared less and less for meat," became very doubtful of the legitimacy of destroying animals for food, and "thought more trouble should be taken to provide the household needs with grains, vegetables, and fruits." When Wyatt Eaton visited him, he took oatmeal and milk for both breakfast and lunch. He didn't feel like eating much in the morning, he said, and if he ate a hearty luncheon it spoiled his appetite for dinner.

Tobacco, however, seems to have tempted him more than alcohol. "I have smoked myself into ill humor, and am peevish and discontented." Once smoking is his "ruling passion," and once at least it is a bad habit, which he must break. He did break it off on numerous occasions, and once he tells Greene how little he misses it. "When one has a bad memory he easily forgets even his vice." But he was never cured for long.

Cigars were his usual diet, but there are a few references to both pipes and cigarettes. Charles Akers, who attended some of the *Divine Comedy* meetings, says, surprisingly, that though Longfellow gave his guests choice cigars, he himself smoked one-cent Salem cheroots. Ernest records a curious story about his giving cigars to young William Winter, who was too much in awe of him to refuse, so that he could only try to smoke them and go out in the garden afterwards to be sick. This suggests an absentmindedness and lack of observation on Longfellow's part far beyond his usual achievements along this line. Yet he never makes a very good case for the use of tobacco, probably because there is none to be made. He disliked persons who smelled of it, and in 1851 he complains of some visitors that "turned my study into a village tavern with cigars and politics, much to my annoyance."

Of the various amusements and occupations that often go along with drinking and smoking Longfellow says little. When he visited Vauxhall in 1835 he thought it "a vulgar place;—had no enjoyment whatever. The only consolation I have is in the thought that I shall never go there again." At the beginning of the Cambridge period, he played whist regularly, once a week, at the Nortons'. Once he speaks of playing whist while others danced. "I like whist to music," he says. There are a number of references to billiards and bowling, but he cared so little for them that I find it delightfully appropriate that he and Tom Appleton should have played billiards "at the Lunatic Asylum" the summer they spent in Brattleboro. In 1858 he himself bought a fine billiard table for his boys, but when it arrived at the Craigie House he regretted it, for there was no place to put it except in his study! "The haunts of the Muses seem invaded by dancing Fauns and Satyrs." There it stayed until the following spring, when, to his "great relief," it was removed to "its new home in the garden."

II

One form of intercourse with his kind—letter-writing—Longfellow disliked, and two others he quite refused. He would not serve on committees, and he would not accept speaking engagements. He was never president of anything except the Dante Society, and this was a mere meeting with his friends. In 1876, when Henry Lee proposed nominating him for the Board of Overseers at Harvard College, he wrote a firm, brief letter in which he begged Lee not to nominate him, and declared without qualification that he would not serve if elected. This decision he had taken "for reasons very conclusive to my own mind."

In the early days, he does not appear to have disliked lecturing, but he got his fill of it during his years as a professor, and when he came to the end of the Harvard road, he rejoiced that it would never be necessary for him to speak in public anywhere again. In 1860 he stayed away from a supper given by the Harvard Musical Association for fear he might be called upon to speak. He did speak at the Whittier Birthday Dinner, but J. T. Trowbridge says he could not be heard. His one notable appearance during his later years was when he read "Morituri Salutamus" at Bowdoin in 1874, and here he was much pleased when he learned that he was to use a high pulpit. "Let me cover myself as much as possible; I wish it might be entirely."

Letter-writing, of course, he could not avoid. I do not know how many letters he wrote, but more than five thousand have been preserved or recorded. For all that, he disliked it and avoided it when he could.

While he is away at college, his mother complains bitterly of his neglect of her. "Do you not love to write *prose?*" To be sure, he also scolds his family for their neglect of him, arguing, with some reasonableness, that they are more to blame than he is, since they can divide the burden, and there is only one of him. Once he excuses himself for not having written because he was so busy reading his sumptuous, newly acquired edition of Chatterton! At least two of his college letters to his father (March 16-23 and December 18, 1824) are mere verbiage, sent, evidently, because they were required, while another (July 22, 1825) is devoted to demonstrating syllogistically that letter-writing is unnecessary and undesirable.

When he went to Europe the first time the situation altered, and he learned what it means to thirst and hunger for a word from home. In the fall of 1826 he gave himself over to such an orgy of letter-writing that one wonders how he found time for anything else, writing enormously long letters, sometimes crossed, sometimes in a microscopic hand bearing no resemblance to his later easy, familiar script. Both varieties remain among his papers to plague the eyesight of posterity.

Insofar as Longfellow had a theory of letter-writing, he expressed it in an 1838 comment on a letter from Sumner "in the epistolary style general." "Oh, give *details* of thy life, dear friend! and not generalities, which nowise satisfy my curiosity." He never changed his mind about this, and toward the end of his life he writes Una Farley that he cannot send her as good a letter as he has received, "for I have not the gift and the grace of letter writing, which are given mostly to women."

Some of his own letters to his family are very stiff. When, in his college days, he corresponds with his mother about the poet Gray, one would fancy he were addressing an academy. He is even more formal in his communications to the family of his first wife, as in the letter he wrote her father after his suit had been accepted, and, even more strikingly, when he reports her death. The euphemistic reference to her miscarriage—"On the night of our arrival the circumstance occurred to which I alluded in my last, and which has had this fatal termination"—sounds especially unnatural today, and his account of her edifying deathbed conversation seems to echo all the worst novels of the period. His prayer beside Mary's body sounds curiously cold also, reflecting an attractive sense of weakness and humility, but with his mind upon himself rather than his dead wife.[4]

Yet there are plenty of authentic nineteenth-century memorabilia which prove beyond question that the worst death-bed scenes in fiction could be paralleled in life, and I am sure that the observations I have just made wrong Longfellow, inevitable as they may seem in our time. What Paul Flemming says in *Hyperion* about certain kinds of poetic diction acting as a barrier between generations applies perfectly here. As a matter of fact, formalized diction is in itself a kind of poetry. Among civilized people, in life as in art, genuine feeling *can* be expressed in highly artificial forms, and this is certainly no less true when the man in question happens to be a professional writer. It would not be safe to conclude that Longfellow did not suffer for the loss of his wife simply because he expressed his grief in what seems to us a stilted or even priggish manner. "Sorrow, and a care that almost killed" he called it in an 1842 sonnet. He was young, and he recovered much more rapidly and completely than he was to recover from the shock of Fanny Appleton's death in 1861. It is clear, too, that his meeting with Fanny aided the process of recovery. But none of this means that his grief was not sincere.

During the years when his eyes were troubling him, letter-writing was a particular burden because it threatened to rob him of the few precious morning hours he tried to hoard for his own writing. Later, after he had become a top-flight celebrity, the Perfect Stranger rained missives upon him in avalanches:

I am overwhelmed with letters on everybody's business but my own. I have a pile like a dirty snowdrift now on my desk, and if postage were one dollar paid in advance, it would be a relief, for it would put a stop to insane and profitless writing, the principal excuse and apology for which seems to be that the writer is an "entire stranger," and therefore &c. &c. &c.

Sometimes—or nearly always—the Perfect Stranger wanted an autograph, which Longfellow sent without question; indeed he seems to have felt that courtesy required him to write a note in which he should say that he was sending the autograph "with pleasure," thus in effect sending two! Even people who afterwards became friends first approached him in this way; E. C. Stedman's first letter was a request for an autograph, not for himself but for a "lady friend" who had "ordered" him to procure one. And, for that matter, both William Winter and James Whitcomb Riley first approached him with requests that he criticize their poems.

But there were people who wanted not one autograph, or two, but a hundred—for charity fairs, and, in one instance at least, for luncheon guests! In 1878 he actually sent a hundred autographs for a fair in Chattanooga, but, as he wrote Robert Winthrop afterwards, he "could not help thinking that the issue of so much paper currency at once would materially affect its value." But the out-and-out lunatics were even worse, and Mrs. Longfellow once wrote Emmeline Wadsworth about a "most desperate love letter" her husband had received from an unknown woman —"a real love letter, though the person knew he was married as was she! but said he could never have found his heart mate, as she implied she had not!" Years later, when he was an old man, a crazy woman telegraphed Longfellow, "If you want to talk with me, come quick to the Briggs House, Forty Second Street, New York." Since he did not want to talk with her, he stayed in Cambridge. "It is pleasant," he remarks primly, "to have such a message read by the gossips at both end of the wire! with both names given in full!"

He was as conscientious as anybody could be about answering letters, for he could not bear to snub anybody, and sometimes he would actually get caught up with his correspondence, but without a secretary, and in pre-typewriter days, it was obviously impossible to stay that way. Once he tells his sister Annie that he has ninety-nine unanswered letters on his desk. His letters are filled with apologies for not having answered sooner, sometimes because of the press of business and sometimes because he had mislaid the letter received and could not find it. On at least one occasion he honored the request of a poetaster to exchange volumes with him! As he was driven to long for storms to keep uninvited visitors from his door, so the only consolation he finds in his final illness is that now at last he can acknowledge letters from strangers with a printed card.

In Longfellow's later years, the situation grew worse instead of better, with "the celebration of my unfortunate birthday by the Schools of the West" and elsewhere. "Fifteen thousand school girls have driven over me. . . . There is no life left in me." Most of these letters came from children, the very last people in the world he wished to wound. One of his very last letters, written in his daughter Annie's hand, only ten days before his death, and signed with his initials, speaks of the "avalanche" of letters precipitated by his seventy-fifth birthday. "Since the first of February, with Annie's assistance I have answered 350 of them and an immense mass still remains unanswered. I sometimes wish that I had taken the ground of not answering any, but that seemed to me too uncivil."

When they appeared in person it was considerably worse than when they came in with letters. What was he to do when a young lady poet arrived "with a manuscript volume . . . in blue velvet" and sat down to read it to him? One "poet" produced an epic of the Creation, "the six days work . . . done up in about six hundred lines." This was at least neat. But what of the other who sent "twenty-eight cantos on an Indian subject, filling an octavo volume of 446 pages," beginning

> My gentle Muse! Awake and sing
> Of wigwam, tomahawk, and quiver?

It was Longfellow's principle never to give criticism, but he often violated it; sometimes he made specific suggestions for revision and improvement, and sometimes he even consented to act as a kind of unofficial author's agent. "It seems to be my destiny," he writes Osgood, "to act as Lord Chamberlain to the ladies, and usher them into the dreadful presence of the Publisher!" [5]

The extent of his thoughtfulness and kindliness in dealing with people who had a halfway reasonable claim upon his attention is illustrated in his correspondence with James Freeman Clarke's daughter Lillian. In 1872 she asked him to look over some Dante drawings. He invites her to the Craigie House on Wednesday afternoon, then adds, "If more convenient for you I would come to town any forenoon, and meet you at Messrs. Osgood & Co.'s at any hour you might prefer." The next day he discovers that he must go into Boston on Wednesday in any event; so he writes her again, inviting her to meet him in town at eleven, to "spare" her "the long journey to Cambridge." At least one later illustrious writer came his way, and it was due to his kind offices that the lady later known as Edith Wharton got some of her early poems published in the *Atlantic*.

This kind of thing was trouble, but there was profit and satisfaction in it too, for such people were worth helping. But what was he to say to those who came asking him for "puffs" or even demanding publication at his expense? One lady brought "three imperial folio volumes of Birds, copied and colored by her own hand from Wilson's ornithology," to ask him "to find some rich man, who would give her three thousand dollars for them." One gentleman took two hours "to explain his system of shorthand writing." And "as he was paralytic in his legs, and had also spine-complaint, and disease of the heart—I could not help listening from compassion."

Sometimes, too, they asked him to put his own pen to work for them. One Western man "ordered" a poem, to be sent with invoice, this last being an item not often requested. One stupid dolt wanted him to write "a poetical epistle" to Jenny Lind, asking charity for him. Always more likely to be indignant in another's behalf than he could be in his own, the poet took the time to make this creature "comprehend the indecency of his behavior," no doubt entirely without success. Howells later recalled being entrusted with escorting one guest to the street car in Harvard Square, with instructions to put him on board, not to leave him until the car started, and then to watch that he didn't get off! But it took extraordinary provocation to drive Longfellow to such lengths. Mere boredom could never do it. As he himself said, he had been bored so often.

His European knowledge, sympathies, and connections greatly enlarged the area of Longfellow's vulnerability. "What you quote about the *père de famille*," he once wrote Sumner, "is pretty true. It is a difficult role to play; particularly when, as in my case, it is united with that of *oncle d'Amérique* and general superintendent of all the dilapidated and tumble-down foreigners who pass this way!" Sometimes they only wanted work, which was reasonable enough, though it was not reasonable to expect him to provide it. Sometimes work was the last thing they wanted. Count Gurowski arrived one day, self-invited, to dinner, remained through supper and until eleven at night, appeared again before sunrise next morning to leave a trifling note, and two days later called a third time, before Longfellow was dressed, to inquire whether the note had been presented. Even after this, the poet offered to lend him money, which he declined, thus showing, his aspiring benefactor thought, "great delicacy of feeling." If so, it was more than most of them showed.

For, like most celebrities, Longfellow had more than his fair share of those unhappy and unfortunate hangers-on who did not want anything in particular except to be themselves, which was quite enough to destroy the peace of life for anybody unfortunate enough to be near them. "One of my crazy women," their victim himself writes; "one of my most intimate bores"; "another bore, who occasionally frequents these forests." Some of them were literally crazy, like the woman who arrived one day, bag and baggage, under the delusion that she was his wife, and had to be carried away by the police. Another woman brought a piano with her that she might sing him a musical setting of one of his poems. Neither must we forget those who addressed him as "General" (perhaps, as he says, confusing him with Washington), or who inquired whether Shakespeare did not live somewhere in the neighborhood, or who asked his age and then informed him that he looked much older. One idiot even informed him that he had died two years before.

Longfellow's unusual gentleness left him particularly vulnerable to this kind of imposition. "Of all the people I ever knew," wrote J. T. Trowbridge, "he was the most charitable in speech, tolerant even of faults which society deems it dangerous to condone." And Elizabeth Stuart Phelps calls him "one of the gentlest men whom I ever knew"; this was more than good breeding, she insists, "because it went beyond and below and above that."

He was no such energetic "do-gooder" as Dickens was, or his friend Samuel Gridley Howe. He lacked the energy for that. But he gave freely to all whom he knew to be in want, and his contacts were wide enough to keep his resources fully employed.[6] Even very benevolent persons have been known to consider the beggars in Italy quite numerous enough, but Longfellow empties alms into the accidentally outstretched hand of a respectable Roman citizen—and is roundly cursed for his pains!

Moreover, his benevolences were coupled with insight and imagination. You did not need to be starving to move him; once he sent $500 to a writer who was in danger of being forced to sell his library. Also, he knew how to give tactfully, without wounding the pride of those who are best worth helping because they will not ask for help. He would ingeniously devise small commissions for people, so that he might seem to be asking favors instead of conferring them, or he might send a New Year's gift to buy gloves with, though he well knew that the money must be spent for more vital necessities.

He knew, too, that want is no respecter of character—or the lack of it—and that even those who deserved their misfortunes might sometimes need to be relieved. "So innate and strong is the love of liberty in all human hearts that, even against our better judgment, we instinctively sympathize with criminals escaping from prison." There was the instructor in his department at Harvard who had to be dismissed for negligence and bad habits. Longfellow does not question the justice of the decision. "Poor fellow! what a life of misery he has led here! Externally a gentleman; but I fear there was always a black spot within." But two days later he is talking, vainly, with President Everett about the possibility of reinstating him.

Sometimes he was taken in and knew it, and, being human, did not enjoy it, as in the case of the German teacher and physician— "poor as a rat"—who brought him a letter from Howe and got money out of him to pay his way to New York, only to go next day to Sumner and make the same plea all over again. The story of the "wounded" Civil War soldier whom he would not help without seeing his wound is generally told as an example of Longfellow's perspicacity, but as Mrs. Fields tells it, the man pretended to have lost a hand at Gettysburg, keeping the stump in his pocket, and Longfellow, all unsuspecting, asked to see it out of genuine sympathetic interest. It is clear that if a mistake had to be made, he always preferred that it should be made at his expense rather than another's. "Why, Charles," he once gently rebuked Norton, "who will be kind to him if I am not?"

Some men succor human need out of a sense of duty, but Longfellow's benevolences were motivated by a genuine, outgoing sympathy toward all sorts and conditions of men. In 1851 a Harvard senior committed suicide, and Longfellow's mind immediately flew off to his parents in New York, who were quite unknown to him personally. "God help them! What a Tragedy!" But pinpricks disturbed him as well as death wounds. In Franconia, New Hampshire, in the summer of 1837, he was greatly distressed lest the innkeeper's wife—"a tall fair girl"—should have overheard a remark of one of the guests concerning the unpalatable dinner she had served. "Poor patient thing! I am sorry from the bottom of my heart!"

It should go without saying that he did not cast off this sensitiveness in his dealings with his own servants. One day, at Nahant, a visitor requested to be enlightened concerning the identity of the lady to whom the poet had just raised his hat upon encountering her in the street. "That," said Longfellow, "is the lady who waited on you at lunch." In London he astonished and amused Browning by passing his umbrella up to the cabby on the box when a shower began suddenly when he and the author of *The Ring and the Book* were out riding together.

Concerning Longfellow's devotion to his friends there has never been any question. Sumner was probably the closest to him—"more like a brother than a friend." But Longfellow's famous reserve did not inhibit warm feelings toward many others. "I should like to know exactly where you are," he writes Lowell in England, "in what street and number, so that I can go in imagination to your door, and see you go out, and in, either in Court dress or otherwise," while Lowell, for his part, looking back over thirty years of friendship, declares that "there has never been a jar between us. If there had been, it would certainly have been my fault and not yours." The noble sonnets, "Three Friends of Mine," transmute Longfellow's gift for friendship into the stuff of fine art.

When his friends could serve him, he did not insult them by neglecting to call upon them, and when he himself was on the giving end, there was no failure to deliver. When young William Winter got the idea that he would like to start a paper in Cambridge, Longfellow offered to finance him. George Washington Greene he served in every way that one man can serve another—with money, with counsel, with comfort, and encouragement. Better still, he brought him into his home, where he humored all his vagaries and performed even physical services for him as patiently as a nurse serves a fretful child. Indeed, Longfellow guarded Greene's interests with more vigilance than his own. When Concord invited him and other distinguished men to help her celebrate the centenary of the battle, he at once requested that, as a distinguished historian, Greene should be invited too.

He also sustained a very close relationship with the German poet Freiligrath, though this had to be carried on entirely through correspondence after Longfellow's return from Europe. "I have just been gazing at your portrait *with considerable tenderness*," he writes in 1843. "God bless you! Be true to yourself, and burn like a watch-fire afar off there in your Germany." In 1848, when there seems a chance that the German liberal may emigrate to America, Longfellow writes, "*The first roof under which you sleep in America must be Washington's—(mine!).*"

After Fanny's death, Longfellow wrote less frequently to Freiligrath, but on May 24, 1867, he found special occasion for a letter. "I have always loved you," he says, "and never for a moment has my feeling abated or changed." And he adds, "I have only just heard of some disasters to your bank, and I venture to come to your aid with the enclosed." But when Freiligrath's son dies in 1873, money cannot help, though sympathy can:

These are the sorrows to which all others are nothing. They change us. We can never be again that we were before, though we may seem so to the eyes of others. But we know that a part of ourselves is gone, and cannot come back again. I will not attempt to console you,—that is useless; but I suffer with you, and share your affliction.

It should be understood clearly that Longfellow's kindness *was* kindness—not weakness. When it was necessary to express an unfavorable judgment or to enter a rebuke, he was quite capable of doing so. Thus he speaks of annuals as "Foundling Hospitals for bastard poetry, the eternal Forget-me-Nots and Souvenirs of the day." *The Ladies' Companion* is such a "milk pan" that he hates to have his work appear in it. Brunswick is "this land of Barbarians—this miserable Down East." In the "great fermenting vats" of the London *Times* "is falsified and adulterated the genuine wine of Truth, as the pure juice of the grape is in the London docks, to fit it for a depraved taste." When Greene wants an American paper in Rome, Longfellow sends him *The New Yorker*. "There is no paper in Boston worth sending." In the election of 1860, he votes early, "but not 'often,' as the Democrats are directed to do." He wonders how a Calvinist dares to beget children when, according to his belief, the chances are all in favor of their being damned. "Ought he not rather go into a Monastery or a Shaker brotherhood, or an Insane Asylum?" But the most amusing statement is at the expense of his own Cambridge, one night in 1870:

The moon is still shining. I looked out of the window just now, and there it was, making my neighbor's house beautiful,—which is more than the architect did. I begin to think that the moon never sets in Cambridge, which accounts perhaps for the number of lunatics here.

Longfellow can be sharp about individuals too, and sometimes in a very picturesque, Dickensian way. Professor Hare, of Philadelphia, is "a well educated bear. I leave you to infer how much I was pleased with shaking a paw with him." Molbach, of the Royal Library, is "a little, awkward man, 'without form and void' —with an enormous head, and lobster eyes," while Rafn is "a tall thin man—with white hair, or rather bristles, standing out in all directions, like a brush; added to which his eyes are always staring wider, so that he looks like a picture of a man who sees a ghost." A European embassy attaché is "a curious looking individual with a horse's head, and mustachios," his resemblance to that animal being the more decided because all the while he was speaking, he "kept his head bobbing about as if he were pulling hay out of the rack." The Irish novelist Lady Morgan, whom he met in 1835, he described as "an elderly lady—dressed young—with a pink robe and turban. Her face is unpleasant—and her whole appearance showy and unrefined." Four days later he encountered her again at Lady Dudley Stuart's—"old and ugly and ill-dressed"—where he also made the acquaintance of a certain Marchioness, "naked almost to the waist; in appearance a magnificent [word erased];

in character, if report be true, no less so; and taken all in all, a superb animal."

In 1846 the historian Prescott appears "drinking his wine freely and with great relish. In any high aims or aspirations he seems entirely wanting." Martin Farquhar Tupper was a "funny little man! quite lifted off his legs with the idea of his fame in this country, and another idea akin to it, that in return he has the whole country under his paternal care and protection. Nothing can be more exquisitely ludicrous, than this whole business!" Henry Ward Beecher, whom Whittier loved, is "clever enough, but to use the native slang phrase, too 'high-faluting.' He is a kind of *Tambour-Major*, and every now and then flourishes his tasselled, silver-headed staff, and the 'great band' strikes up with all its wind-instruments." In 1856, having entertained his friends George William Curtis and Bayard Taylor, he says that they are "Lecturers, and at present see the world from that point of view." In 1858, Edward Everett remarks that he has just signed a certain petition. "I could hardly refrain," says Longfellow, "from asking him if he 'signed it without reading it,' or 'under the effects of an anodyne,' as he said at the South he had done the Sumner testimonial, the coward!" Even to the end, the capacity for sharp judgment was there. In August 1881 he heard Wendell Phillips at the Harvard Commencement. "Yes," he said, as he was leaving the stage, "it was marvellous and delightful, but preposterous from beginning to end."

As we have already seen, Longfellow was loyal to his friends: he once threatened to walk out at a Boston dinner table where Sumner was being criticized. Even Nathan Appleton's house was closed to Sumner following his controversy with Winthrop over slavery and the Mexican War, but this did not affect the attitude of either Longfellow or his wife toward Sumner in any way.[7] But the poet was honest with his friends too, and it was always clear that he had given neither his judgment nor his conscience into their keeping. Once he apologized to Sam Ward for "my most ungracious way of receiving your New Year's Present: the 'Yellow Book'; you know I feel your kindness in sending it; but as I have neither interest in it nor respect for the author, I thought I would be frank enough to say so." He could chide good-humoredly, too, when chiding seemed in order, as when he wrote his brother Sam asking him to bring a legal paper—"Don't leave it on the table, as you did the eight dollars, some cents, of the French Note Paper purchase!" and again, a month later, when he sent a note after him, which "came just as you left us—just as you were walking away with my india rubbers!"

Longfellow's letters to Greene are particularly interesting in this connection, for they show that in spite of all his patience with his friend's vagaries, he was fully aware of them. More than once he chides Greene for the brevity of his letters. "Write me very soon—immediately—and as I never make any marginal notes in your letters, you need not trouble yourself to leave a margin." The letter he wrote Greene on July 23, 1839, is perhaps Longfellow's longest letter; certainly it is one of the sharpest. In microscopic hand writing he gets the equivalent of over ten pages of double-spaced typing on one four-page sheet. The letter begins:

Yours of May 22 arrived two or three days ago. I was glad to get it although there was literally nothing in it. Your "turn" to complain; as if you ever did anything but complain! Three pages of fault-finding you call a letter. I don't hang such letters. Find fault to your heart's content! But be more concentrated.... As to asking any human being to put those 8vo volumes (Prescott's Hist. for instance) into his trunk, and take them through England and France into Italy is what I will not do even for you.

"What a coward you are in some things," he writes Greene in 1867, though he adds, "I dare say in similar circumstances I should be a greater one." Sometimes, even, he seems to have indicated his awareness of Greene's peculiarities to others, as when he writes to his sister-in-law about "my friend Greene ... who I believe gets a part of everything going, and first or last has had all calamities. Nothing remains for him, but to be struck by lightning; and this Summer he will have a good chance for that, as we have on an average one thunderstorm a day."

Collectively, men seem to have interested Longfellow less than individually. In politics as a science he took no interest whatever: "I must confess I care but little about politics or anything of the kind, and therefore read and know but very little about them, so that the columns of my paper devoted to political speculations are to me almost as uninteresting as so many columns of the tradesmen's advertisements." This is an utterance of youth, but the tone does not change greatly during later years. In 1849 he reports Sumner and Hillard as "working in separate shafts of the dark dirty political coal mine." In '56 he fails to enjoy a dinner because the conversation was political. "It was not until after dinner, in the library, that we got upon anything really interesting." And as late as '73 he complains to Greene that Sumner is sending him "nothing but newspapers, and those dreary Public Documents, the necessity of whose existence in print I do not clearly see." It is interesting to remember that Sumner himself always found the Craigie House a refuge from the political strife into which he had been led by his conscience and his sense of public duty much more than by his tastes or ambitions.

Longfellow voted religiously, out of his sense of obligation, but he did not relish even that much political activity. "Voted, and came home to sit by the fireside and read poetry and forget politics." He never attended a political caucus until 1870. As to running for public office, the very idea horrified him, as he made abundantly clear in 1844, when Whittier wished him to stand for Congress as the Liberty Party candidate. In 1861 Longfellow wanted Sumner as Minister to England and was indignant when Lincoln failed to make the appointment. Four years later, he urged Sumner to use his influence to send Lowell to Switzerland. But in neither case did he exert himself directly. The whole atmosphere of political action distressed his gentle and fastidious spirit, and he shuddered to see Emerson, in Fugitive Slave days, "hissed and hooted at by young law-students."

Lawrance Thompson has scolded Longfellow for his political indifferentism during his first visit to Europe, and his tendency to lose himself instead in scholarship and the romantic past. Herein, I fear, his historic sense fails him. Longfellow's business in Europe was language and literature, not revolutionary activity; the Continent seemed very remote from practical American interests in the 1820's, and it is hardly fair to ask a young man of that happier and more sensible age to take on all the problems of meddling Americans of the mid-twentieth century in addition to his own.

As a matter of fact, Longfellow was not lacking in a reasonable social consciousness. As early as 1838, he urged Greene not to spend all his time in Italy digging up the past with a living and vital people swarming all about him. He rejoiced in the revolutions of 1848, and if he was too hospitable to the comfortable notion that utopia would turn the corner just as soon as the world had got rid of kings, that was the myopia of the age. He rejoiced when the Prussians dethroned their king, when the Austrians were driven out of Lombardy, and when the French failed to take Rome. Louis Napoleon disgusted him, but Americans who admired Louis Napoleon disgusted him more. He entertained Kossuth when the Hungarian patriot visited America in 1851, and greatly admired him; at the same time, he was intelligent enough to perceive that we ought not, through sympathy, abandon our time-tested policy of non-intervention in the affairs of other nations.[8]

On the home front, he praised Thoreau's account of his spending a night in jail rather than pay a poll tax to finance the Mexican War. His lifelong sympathy with Indians, expressed in *Hiawatha* and elsewhere, and foreshadowed when he took part in a college debate, was, like Cooper's, influenced by the writings of the kindly Moravian missionary John Heckewelder, who, through his influence on Conrad Richter, is still moulding American literature in our own time. Like his mother before him, he disbelieved in capital punishment—

> Ah! it is the gallows-tree!
> Breath of Christian charity,
> Blow, and sweep it from the earth!—

and after Garfield's assassination he feared "some popular outbreak of vengeance" against the murderer.[9] He had no feeling of superiority toward those who labor; the poem "To a Child" ponders, among other things, the possibility of his growing up to work with his hands, and this is not viewed as an unhappy fate. He believed that "the true mission of this country is to receive the poor and the degraded of all countries and teach them to be men," and that our real danger came "not from the poor, but from the rich and corrupt, who bring the pest not in their ragged clothes, but in their ragged opinions." [10]

Of course the great political cause of Longfellow's day was emancipation. He was an antislavery man always, though not an abolitionist; when he associated with abolitionists, he felt like "Alfred among the Danes." He favored Elihu Burritt's plan of compensated emancipation, and once at least he went so far as to call Garrison "a Traitor to his country" whom he "cannot forgive."

His zeal for slavery reform even overcame, in a measure, his lack of interest in voting and his dislike of political meetings. In his youth he contemplated a play on Toussaint L'Ouverture. This never materialized, but he did speak out in the *Poems on Slavery*. Now that the smoke of the conflict has blown away, these are often spoken of as "milk-and-water stuff." As Longfellow himself says, "They are written in a kindly—not a vindictive spirit." But in a day when the book could not be reviewed in *Graham's Magazine* because the word slavery was itself taboo in its columns, it took courage to write them nevertheless; moreover Longfellow allowed the New England Anti-Slavery Association to reprint the collection for distribution in the very region where it could most damage the sale of his books. Nor should it be forgotten that Whittier was enough satisfied with *Poems on Slavery* to desire Longfellow to run for Congress on an antislavery platform.

Like the rest of New England, Longfellow was shocked by

Daniel Webster's tendencies toward compromise with the slave power, though he was certainly less intemperate in expressing his displeasure than many Yankees were, and disapproved of those who spoke harshly of the great statesman forever after, even at the time of his death. But when Eliot of Boston voted for the Fugitive Slave Bill, Longfellow thought the city disgraced. "If we should read in Dino Compagni that in the tenth century a citizen of Florence had given such a vote, we should see what an action he had done." When the slave-hunters come to Boston, he longs to throw them into prison When Massachusetts men break the law, he is pleased, and he certainly overpraises John Brown. "This government must not pass laws that outrage the sense of right in the community."

As early as 1854, Longfellow found himself uncomfortable while entertaining two Southern clergymen, even though they said nothing about slavery. And despite all his reluctance to engage in personal controversy, he could not restrain himself in the presence of the Florida judge who argued that "do unto others" meant merely that you must treat your slaves as you would wish to be treated if you were a slave. "If you were a slave," said Longfellow bluntly, "the thing you would wish most of all would be your freedom. So your Scripture argument for Slavery is knocked into a cocked hat." And the judge blushed and laughed and admitted defeat.

In the course of time, however, the antislavery cause unhappily linked itself with the war cause, and this involved a conflict in Longfellow's sympathies. For though no American poet had a more glamorous military background than Longfellow, none ever more hated war. Elihu Burritt, who was an excellent judge in these matters, placed Longfellow ahead of all other Americans as a peace poet. He was not a pacifist in the doctrinaire sense of the term, as Whittier was. Yet Whittier has more provocative utterances to his credit in the Civil War crisis than Longfellow has.

William Longfellow, the poet's first American ancestor, died in 1690, in Sir William Phips's expedition against Quebec. As has already been stated, he himself was named for a naval hero. The War of 1812 brought prosperity back to Portland after Jefferson's embargo had destroyed it, and the sea fight commemorated in "My Lost Youth" brought sounds of battle within the hearing range of its inhabitants. Nothing could have been better calculated than these things to stir the martial ardors of a child. Henry's very first letter to his father in January 1814 asks for the gift of a drum from Boston, though he courteously places his sister's request for a Bible first. His grandfather General Peleg Wadsworth's house in the forests of Maine was a kind of fort, and the old man's stories of days gone by enthralled the little boy's imagination.

But when he became a man he put away childish things. It is true that at one time there was some half-serious thought of sending him to West Point, and there was one rather hypochondriacal moment during his Bowdoin career when he wondered whether it would not have been better if he had gone there, on the not overwhelmingly patriotic ground that it might have benefited his health. During his college days, the Bowdoin Cadets ran through a brief career, and this was his only contact with military drill. Many years later he exerted his own objections to keep Ernest out of West Point.

All this was not wholly a revolt against environment. Longfellow's mother, general's daughter though she was, was intensely antimilitaristic, and his father opposed peacetime conscription. Moreover, even General Wadsworth was far from being a fire-eater. As a boy he was so fond of learning that he walked eight miles to attend school. When he himself taught, he used military drill but abolished harsh discipline and used "advanced" teaching methods for his day. He disliked "hellfire" sermons also and allowed his own children a larger-than-average amount of freedom in the home.

Even in the Spanish romances, peace appealed to Longfellow more than war. Both he and Fanny disliked the heavy fighting in the *Iliad*. His first published poem, "The Battle of Lovell's Pond," was on a military theme, but except for "The Cumberland" and "A Ballad of the French Fleet," he did little to exploit this vein afterwards. "I am afraid I could hardly use Mr. Simms' war poems," he writes Paul Hamilton Hayne, while working on his *Poems of Places*. "I may have to insert some few pieces of the kind, but they will be as few as possible, and not of the fiercest."

The Pilgrim life depicted in *The Courtship of Miles Standish* has its military side:

> Giants in heart were they, who believed in God and the Bible,—
> Ay, who believed in the smiting of Midianites and Philistines.

When Wattawamat's head

> Scowled from the roof of the fort, which at once was a church and a fortress,
> All who beheld it rejoiced, and praised the Lord, and took courage.

All, that is, except Priscilla, a true Longfellow heroine:

> Only Priscilla averted her face from this spectre of terror,
> Thanking God in her heart that she had not married Miles Standish.

Thor's challenge to Christ in "The Saga of King Olaf" is plainly dramatic, and it was largely an accident that "Paul Revere's Ride," appearing in the *Atlantic* at the beginning of the Civil War, should have stimulated the martial spirit of the hour. In the early "Hymn of the Moravian Nuns of Bethlehem," the banner being made is a standard for General Pulaski, but the poem culminates in a plea for mercy upon vanquished foes. "The Arsenal at Springfield," written at the suggestion of Mrs. Longfellow and widely circulated by the English Peace Society, is a powerful antiwar poem, and Gitchi Manito's attitude toward war in *Hiawatha* is anything but friendly. In *Kavanagh* the preacher who offers prayers on horseback at the general muster of the militia, and delights in "going quite at large into some of the bloodiest campaigns of the ancient Hebrews" is pretty roughly handled. The Civil War itself produced "Christmas Bells," an assertion of faith in life despite the horrors of the conflict and, later, both the austere "Killed at the Ford," which concerns the senseless waste of war and the sufferings it inflicts, especially upon women, and a musing piece called "A Nameless Grave," which expresses the humility that any sensitive man must feel before one who has given everything he had for a cause.

Longfellow himself faced the challenge of a war situation first at the time of the Mexican War, a "shabby" and "disgraceful" affair. He was proud when his brother Sam prayed in the pulpit for the "country in her hour of shame" and sent one "patriotic" member of the congregation stamping his way out up the aisle. In 1847 he complained of the "intellectual legerdemain" which, in wartime, makes murder "glory instead of crime."

The Civil War was more difficult. From the beginning Longfellow opposed appeasing the South: "The reign of old Buchanan and the rest of them begins today. A poor piece of business at best. Before long we shall have a bad state of things, imbecility on horseback."

He believed in Lincoln from his nomination. "I am feeling very well," he wrote his sister on election day, "and full of faith in the triumph of the good cause, to which you and I belong." And there is an undated letter fragment in which he says, "When I next write I hope to tell you that Abraham Lincoln is Patriarch of America."

Between Lincoln's election and his inauguration, Longfellow's attitude toward the South grew sterner. On December 20 he is afraid not that the Southern states will go but that the North will yield. On January 29, "the six fugitive states" remind him of "six paupers leaving the Union Workhouse." On February 6 he finds that fear is the only thing he is afraid of. "Seward and Adams have done wrong in suggesting such a thing as compromise, under present circumstances; and it discourages the friends of freedom." The inaugural address itself he thought "conciliatory and yet firm."

Does this mean that Longfellow had already made up his mind to accept civil war to preserve the Union? This question is difficult to answer. His brother Sam, who, having a more doctrinaire mind than his brother, could generally formulate his position upon such questions with greater definiteness, wrote Fanny from Florence in February:

For my part I long to have the Slave States go: I would give them forts, arsenals, custom houses, and mints if they would really and positively go. I long to see the Free States accept this providentially offered opportunity of emancipating themselves from their long irksome bondage to such arrogant masters, and still more from their moral complicity in the guilt of slavery.

There is no suggestion in this letter that at the time Samuel Longfellow had even considered the possibility of war.

But when Sumter was fired upon, Longfellow knew that the hour had come—"the impending doom of a nation." Even now, what impresses him is "the sadder aspect"—the youngsters in uniform guarding the State House, and destined for God only knew what. He reassures himself that the North could not have prevented the war, and he is already very impatient with "John Bull" for putting "Civilization and Barbarism" on a plane of equality. Already, too, the martial spirit is beginning to sicken him, and he is exceedingly tired of war sermons. "A 'truce of God' once a week is pleasant. At present the North is warlike enough, and does not need rousing." He kept Charley out of the war until he ran away, and he kept Ernest out altogether—"he thought one of his children risking his life was enough"—though he did yield sufficiently to the "practical" spirit of the times to have him enrolled in the Lawrence Scientific School instead of Harvard College.

He might have been pardoned surely if he had tried to ignore the war, for his own Calvary came upon him, with the tragic death of his wife, just as the darkness was engulfing the nation. As a matter of fact, however, little distortion can be observed, for his reactions to the war are just what might have been expected of a man of his background, convictions, and temperament. Though he was displeased with several of Lincoln's appointments, he hailed the Emancipation Proclamation, found the Gettysburg Address admirable, and breathed more freely when Lincoln had been re-elected. Ben Butler's activities in New Orleans earned the sobriquet "General Attila Barbarossa Butler." Perhaps his most considered utterance on the war in general was written to Bernhard Roelker:

Meanwhile the great war goes thundering on. I hope you are cheery about it, and have faith in something and somebody. The slave-power must be utterly annihilated. There can be no peace without that done; and for that I devoutly pray. A pseudo-aristocracy based on the theory that "a black man has no rights which a white man is bound to respect" cannot any longer be tolerated.

After the war, Longfellow supported Sumner's Reconstruction policy and had many harsh things to say about President Johnson, "a terrible old man of the sea to have on our shoulders for three years." Johnson, who achieved "a general jail delivery of every scoundrel in the country," proved, he thought, "that the 'poor whites' of the South 'ne sont pas du bois dont on fait les bons Présidents.' " Later, the scandals of the 'seventies, crying out for a Juvenal, depressed him deeply, "the terrible revelations of corruption at Washington." He attributed these defalcations to "sowing gunpowder" and wondered whether we were not becoming "the most dishonest nation on the face of the earth," and he felt too that the Republican Party might well ponder the case of the man who "thought he was only committing murder, but found it was suicide." But this time he refused to follow Sumner's leadership in deserting Grant for Greeley, consistently maintaining that "even admitting the truth of the allegations against the present administration, I still fear that the country is far safer in its hands than it would be in those of its opponents."

CHAPTER THREE

"Books were his passion and delight"

I

So far we have been concerned with Longfellow as a man and have given our attention to his general human qualities. But he was also a poet, a scholar, and a teacher, and it is now time to turn to these more specialized and individualized qualities.

The Student in the *Tales of a Wayside Inn* has clearly been modeled upon Chaucer's Clerk, but Longfellow could just as well have been describing himself:

> Books were his passion and delight,
> And in his upper room at home
> Stood many a rare and sumptuous tome,
> In vellum bound, with gold bedight,
> Great volumes garmented in white,
> Recalling Florence, Pisa, Rome.

Precious books, that is, like Longfellow's own set of the Bodoni Dante, which he found in Italy, lacking one volume, only to encounter the stray afterwards in an obscure shop in Boston. "He enjoyed handsome bindings and fine paper," writes Alice Longfellow, "and took pains to cut the pages with the utmost nicety and precision. An ill-cut, rough edge was a positive pain to him."

The dispersal of the Prescott library saddened him: the massacre of the poets, he called it.

It is true that in his old age there were times when Longfellow satisfied himself by marking the catalogues but not sending in the order. All in all, however, the found book-collecting the most fascinating way of spending money that man has devised, and the last of our passions to leave us. But before proceeding to a systematic survey of his reading, let us glance briefly as his experience of the nonliterary arts.

Of architecture little need be said. Though he permits Michael Angelo to call it the greatest of the arts, Longfellow himself has little to say about it. The few comments he does make all concern the Gothic, and all deal with spiritual meanings; there is no technical study whatever. His first Gothic cathedral was Rouen, and his imagination was "completely overwhelmed" by its "impression of awful sublimity." He was almost equally enthusiastic about Strasbourg, and he felt it necessary to restrain his raptures over York when he was sixty. In the second of the sonnets inspired by *The Divine Comedy*, he achieved a notable poetic expression of the emotions which Gothic architecture inspired in him.

There is more about statues, paintings, and *objets d'art*. That Longfellow was fond of all these is attested by the number he collected. He seems to have felt that sculpture was nobler and more substantial than painting. During his first trip abroad he praised the Venus of Canova above the Venus of Medici, possibly because it is more modest. He was also greatly impressed by the veiled statuary at the Chapel of St. Severus in Naples, which he describes in some detail.

He was not inclined to award the Greeks unquestioned supremacy, though he admired many Greek works—for one, "the athletic Sleeping Faun of Praxiteles." On the other hand, he calls Dannecker's Ariadne superior to the Venus of Medici. Naturally this tendency on Longfellow's part did not make him less appreciative of the work of contemporary American sculptors. It is true that he was "a good deal disappointed" in his first view of the Greek Slave of Hiram Powers—he does not say why—but he was strongly impressed by the same sculptor's Proserpine and by Crawford's Orpheus. He also admired Harriet Hosmer, one of whose busts is still in the Longfellow House, where one variety of visitor still sometimes inquires whether it represents "one of Mr. Longfellow's daughters."

It will be perceived that these are all lay judgments. The same is true of what he says about paintings. He admired Rosa Bonheur for her "truth to nature." He praised Doré's pictures for the "Inferno" but pronounced Darley's fine line drawings for "Rip Van Winkle" "meagre and insufficient." On a portfolio of Rembrandt etchings he made the perfect layman's comment: "What homely women! and yet how true to nature." According to Blanche Roosevelt, he was quite unimpressed by his son Charley's collection of Japanese pictures, which he thought "more comical than beautiful." The same writer quotes his enthusiastic praise of David's picture of the death of Queen Elizabeth I:

The terror and agony depicted on the countenance are so natural as to be alarming; the hard face of the queen, while retaining all of its usual characteristics, wears also a new expression of humility that lessens the general repulsiveness and reflects wonderful credit on the able pencil of the painter.

If this seems to reflect a stronger appetite for realism than Longfellow usually manifests, the moral significance he discerned—or read into—the picture may well be responsible. In general he disliked pictures of modern life, finding "our fatal broadcloth" ill adapted to the painter's brush.

There is more to say about music, which began for him in the home. As we have already seen, his mother pictures him, at eight months, as "an active rogue," who "wishes for nothing so much as singing and dancing." He learned to play both the piano and the flute,[1] and there is an 1843 letter in which Mrs. Longfellow speaks of his playing a nocturne for her. Alice says that he played by ear, "and would often pass the twilight hours at the piano, recalling bits from favorite operas." In his old age he gave "music lessons" to his little grandson, and Mrs. Fields says that he used to enjoy singing under his breath, in his box at the opera.

During his early years his music was largely operatic. "Noisy Oratorios" had been spoiled for him by bellowing church choirs, and apparently Handel had suffered somewhat from the same cause. It was very different with Mozart, whose *Marriage of Figaro* was his favorite opera. He encountered both *Figaro* and *Don Giovanni* in April 1836, and though he disliked the Don's book, he was enraptured by the music. That same year he first heard both *Der Freischütz* and *Les Huguenots* also. The former he thought "loud, thundering music" compared to Mozart—"no music but noise"—but he admits he heard a poor performance. The *Huguenots* music, on the other hand, was "grand," but he was unable to work up any interest in the story and went home early. In 1847 he went to *Norma* two successive nights, and in 1852 he was charmed by *La Favorita,* though amused by the young Frenchman behind him who thought it superior to *Don Giovanni.*

Rigoletto came along in 1854; Longfellow thought it "wild music but very stirring." By 1857 *Fidelio* had already become "simple and beautiful, and old-fashioned." In 1859 he found *Martha* "charming. Light, aerial, graphic music," but in 1861 he pronounces *A Masked Ball* both "new and null." He heard some Wagner in concert as early as 1853, finding it "strange, original, and somewhat barbaric," but in 1877 he wrote Elizabeth Stuart Phelps very enthusiastically about *Lohengrin.* In his later years, he did not think he cared for the "new" opera, but he was not intolerant of it, for he admired Boïto's *Mefistofele,* though with some reservations.

Among comic operas, he was devoted, in later years, to *Pinafore,* but he thought *The Beggar's Opera* "interesting chiefly from its historical associations." [2]

Perhaps Longfellow's comments on singers are more interesting than what he says about the operas themselves. Like so many of the mid-century intellectuals, he was quite captivated by Jenny Lind. He attended her first Boston concert on September 27, 1850, when he paid $8.50 for his ticket and sat in the gallery. "She is very feminine and lovely," he told his journal. "Her power is in her presence, which is magnetic, and takes her audience captive before she opens her lips. She sings like the morning star; clear, liquid, heavenly sounds." The next year, after hearing her sing the "Deh vieni" of his beloved *Figaro,* he begged Sumner, "if ever you see it advertised, and she to sing it, do not fail to go, though the Union be in danger." And he adds, "Love, tenderness, longing, never found a more complete and triumphant expression than in that music, and Jenny's face while singing it!" He heard her on a number of occasions, in good voice and bad, and after her last concert in 1851, he lamented that he could "never hear that voice divine any more, nor see that radiant face again!" By this time, however, he had decided that she had "a Northern soul" and sang Northern music better than Southern. He also met her, as he met all celebrities who came to Boston. "There is something very fascinating about her; a kind of soft wildness of manner, and sudden pauses in her speaking, and floating shadows over her face."

For all his admiration of Jenny Lind's spiritual quality, Longfellow did not disparage her great rival, Giulia Grisi, as Lind's admirers were often inclined to do. In January 1855 he found himself going to hear her and Mario every night; "the Queen of the Lyric Drama" he calls her. He had enjoyed Henrietta Sontag in Paris in the 'twenties, and when she came to Boston in the 'fifties he enjoyed her again, for she was still a fine artist, though with her voice "a little faded." When he first encountered the sixteen-year-old Patti, in *The Barber of Seville,* in 1860, he thought her "crude, but full of promise," though "too young to appear on the stage." Two weeks later he admits that he "never saw a better Amina." He took a great interest in the American soprano Clara Louise Kellogg, whom he seems to have heard first in 1861. At the beginning of the 'seventies, another charming nightingale, Christine Nilsson, came out of the north. He thought her "sunny, fresh, and beautiful," and "liked herself even better than her singing." The year 1879 brought Etelka Gerster—"a divine singer. Her pure, young, fresh soprano voice is exquisite"—and another

American, Minnie Hauk, in a new opera, *Carmen,* which he thought "rather brilliant."

Among the instrumentalists, there is a slighting reference to Paganini, in Dresden, in 1829. Later Schlesinger, de Meyer, Thalberg, Rubinstein, and Ole Bull are all spoken of admiringly. Ole Bull became a personal friend and suggested the Musician in *Tales of a Wayside Inn.* He was also acquainted with Liszt and commissioned a portrait of him by Healy, which still hangs in the Longfellow House.[3] I get the impression that Longfellow's interest in instrumental music increased during his later years, but I believe his greatest enthusiasm was always reserved for the voice. Once he speaks very enthusiastically of a chamber music concert, and once he finds an organ recital of Bach fugues and preludes "learned and . . . decidedly heavy." Though there are two enthusiastic references to Beethoven's Ninth, his son-in-law says he never cared greatly for symphony concerts.

There was little theater in Portland during Longfellow's youth, but there were no prejudices against it in the Longfellow household, and the children went to circuses and menageries too when they could get there. Longfellow did not scorn the humbler branches of theatrical entertainment during his later years either, and Elizabeth Stuart Phelps has recorded how he wept over a performance of *Hazel Kirke.*

It was Longfellow's considered opinion that Rachel was the greatest actress he ever saw. He knew and admired Modjeska, Adelaide Neilson, and Mary Anderson, but he seems cold to New England's own greatest actress, Charlotte Cushman—"I like less acting better" [4]—and he records having seen Matilda Heron without making any comment on her. Ernest Longfellow records the legend that Sarah Bernhardt kissed his father when she came to see him, but refuses to vouch for its authenticity. Let us hope that this was not the reason why Longfellow failed to attend Madame Sarah's performances when she was in Boston again at the very end of his life.

Among the men, he admired such varied performers as Edwin Booth, Salvini, and Charles Mathews, though he objected to

Booth's mutilation of *The Taming of the Shrew*, which transformed it "from a Comedy into a romping Farce." He defended Edwin Forrest's Lear against Mathews's criticism of it. Charles Fechter's Hamlet he calls "very unconventional,—natural, easy. . . . It is pleasant to see anything like nature on the stage; not the everlasting mouthing and ranting." This was quite in line with Dickens's appreciation of Fechter and may have been influenced by Dickens, but it was also in line with Longfellow's own taste.

He did not care much for anybody who split the ears of the groundlings. Charles Kean as a man was "pleasant and modest"; on the stage he was "a fine ranter with a bad voice." Vandenhoff read Hamlet's lines well but he had "too many claptraps and tricks for a great actor." This kind of thing was even more annoying in less classical types of play: Lester Wallack as Don Caesar de Bazan "grimaced too much; and overdid the matter in the English style." Longfellow thought Dion Boucicault's *The Siege of Lucknow* "pretty poor, and dull, though with some scenic effect," and Alice Longfellow has recorded that she was furious with her father for laughing at her raptures over *The Lady of Lyons*.

It is not surprising, then, that Longfellow should have sympathized with Howells's attempts to bring in a more "natural" type of play. He was much interested when Lawrence Barrett produced *A Counterfeit Presentment* and entertained both the author and the actor at the Craigie House. "If . . . [Howells] can make people listen to comedies of character instead of incident, it will be a revolution in matters theatrical." [5]

One of Longfellow's special dramatic enthusiasms was for the Shakespearean "readings" of Fanny Kemble. Since the great English actress was a beloved friend both to him and to Mrs. Longfellow, his social and aesthetic values are very closely intermingled at this point. Indeed, Mrs. Longfellow had played Olivia to Mrs. Kemble's Viola in 1839, before her marriage to Longfellow, in a series of tableaux given at Lenox, Massachusetts.

Longfellow admits that Fanny Kemble's red-covered reading desk looked like "the gory block on the scaffold," and, like Dickens, he objected to her pronunciation of "Henery" in Shake-speare's historical plays, but both his journals and Mrs. Longfel-low's contain many enthusiastic comments upon the readings in general. He preferred her tragedy to her comedy, though making an exception of *Twelfth Night*, and during her Boston "farewell" in 1859, he thought both the *Lear* and the *Antony and Cleopatra* "stupendous."

One night in 1850, Fanny Kemble created a sensation when, after a Boston reading of *As You Like It*, she surprised and thrilled her great audience by reciting "The Building of the Ship," "standing out upon the platform, book in hand, trembling, palpi-tating, and weeping, and giving every word its true weight and emphasis." It must have been one of the great nights of Longfel-low's life, though he characteristically says little about his own emotions. But he had already paid his tribute to the actress in his "Sonnet on Mrs. Kemble's Readings from Shakespeare," which he presented to her at a supper in the Craigie House, following one of her performances.

II

Longfellow makes surprisingly few references to reading the Bible, though his poems present abundant evidence of his famil-iarity with it. Once he speaks of his wife reading him "the ever-beautiful story of Joseph," and once he awards "the purer and brighter waters" of the Scriptures the palm over the pagan classics. Horace he calls his "favorite classic," as indeed he ought to have been, for Horace got his academic career for him and saved him from the law. J. P. Pritchard finds numerous resemblances be-tween Horace and Longfellow, both in theory and in practice. He mentions Xenophon, Livy, and Ovid, and in 1870 a week of Plautus left him very tired of "pimps, parasites, and debauchery in general." He read more of the Church Fathers than might have been expected of a nontheological scholar. His Latin seems to have been better than his Greek,[6] but in 1839 we find him reading the Greek poets for an hour every morning, and later he writes Sam Ward of having read "the tenth chapter of Mark in Greek." In

1858 he comments unenthusiastically on the *Agamemnon* of Aes-
chylus: "Cassandra's prophetic frenzy is grand, and so is the cry
of the murdered King from within. But the whole seems to me
heavy and obscure." Like Dickens, he was devoted to *The Arabian Nights*, and Newton Arvin found that "images from that
work arose in his mind, when he was deeply moved, without his
summoning them consciously."

Naturally he has much more to say about English literature.
His comments on Anglo-Saxon matters are mostly those of the
professional scholar. Barring a few not very significant references
to Chaucer, he does not, *as a reader*, seem to have very much to
say about the pre-Elizabethans.

Most of his references to Shakespeare deal with the various
performances he witnessed. Once he attempts a typical nineteenth-
century interpretation of *The Tempest* in allegorical terms, and
once he notes having read in the *Gesta Romanorum* the "idle tale"
of Apollonius of Tyre, "on which Shakespeare founded *The
Tempest*." This of course is a slip for *Pericles*. Once he wondered
why Shakespeare called a play *Love's Labour's Lost* "when it was
not lost after all." When his wife read *The Merchant of Venice*
to him, Portia reminded him of Julia Ward Howe, and he was
impressed too by the "perfect representation of a southern summer night" in the last act, which seemed all the more remarkable
since Shakespeare never saw Italy.

An unnamed newspaper correspondent has recorded that Longfellow preferred Leigh Hunt's sonnets to Shakespeare's. If this is
correctly reported, perhaps Longfellow's interest in the Italian
form of the sonnet, as witnessed by his own practice, supplies the
reason. The judgment is easier to credit in view of a disappointed
reading of Shakespeare's sonnets as recorded in Longfellow's
journal of 1840: "Either I was not wholly awake to their beauties,
or those beauties have been exaggerated." Two years later he
seems to put them higher by implication when he speaks of
Wordsworth's sonnets as the next best.

The University of Pennsylvania has three letters from Longfellow to Dr. Horace Howard Furness,[7] who had sent the poet his

great "New Variorum" edition of *Hamlet;* Longfellow is decorous and appreciative but says nothing that is not thoroughly conventional. He thought Furness's quotations from Elze showed him "to be of a more sane mind" than many of the others. A more extended comment on *Hamlet* shows Longfellow responsive to its literary grandeur but distressed by the "savage and ferocious taste" of our ancestors as reflected by the orgy of killing. "It is as bad as the taste of the Spaniard for a Bullfight," he says, which would seem to reflect an unfortunate confusion between art and life.

There is not much on the other Elizabethans. An undated manuscript lecture on Goethe yields a slighting reference to Marlowe's *Dr. Faustus,* "a very meagre thing." One rainy day in 1859 Longfellow read *The Virgin Martyr* of Massinger: "Like all the old dramatists, too much in 'the great bow-wow style.' But in all these scenes where Dorothea appears, it is very beautiful, with lofty spiritual meaning." *The Faerie Queene* lay more within his range, and he read it "with infinite delight." He imitated Lyly's Euphuistic style in Chipsa's speeches in *The Spanish Student.* He admired Sir Philip Sidney. Though Lowell was not quite able to convince him that "Going to Bed" was an innocent poem, his appreciation of Donne was not contemptible for his time.

He had no serious doubts of Milton's greatness, though he once calls *Samson Agonistes* dull. Dryden he praised for his "strong, deep-sea atmosphere," but "theological discussion in verse," carried to the length of "The Hind and the Panther," did not appeal to him. The Songs and Elegies he found "pretty tame sometimes; and then will come a line which flashes across the page like a train of powder."

Wordsworth's *Prelude* "soars and sinks, and is by turns sublime and commonplace." His "Laodamia" Longfellow found out of keeping in parts. A Grecian hero would hardly talk in such a strain of nineteenth-century moralizing. Longfellow's relish of the immortality ode was only lessened by his reluctance to believe that we all possess "only second-hand souls." In his paper on "The Defence of Poetry" he saw Wordsworth as in some aspects a useful antidote to Byronism. He burlesqued Byronic gloom in *Kavanagh* in the person of Mr. H. Adolphus Hawkins, Poet. But he had no desire "to make a bugbear of Lord Byron's name, nor figuratively to disturb his bones," and there is evidence to show that he carried *Childe Harold's Pilgrimage* about Europe with him. He says nothing of significance about the other Romantic poets, though he does remark of Shelley that "there are certain moods which his poetry meets and satisfies more than any other," and when he reports the death of his first wife to Ticknor, he quotes from, and modifies, "Adonais":

> Peace! peace! She is not dead! She does not sleep!
> She has awakened from the dream of life.[8]

He was a great enthusiast for Tennyson. *In Memoriam* interested him as much as if he had written it himself, and the *Idylls of the King* were hailed as "King Alfred's new volume" and "worthy to hang beside The Faerie Queene." In an undated 1850 letter, Mrs. Longfellow speaks of his reading *In Memoriam* "with eyes full of tears" and herself looks forward to reading it at Nahant, "with the melancholy sea chiming in as music to the dirge-like words." He admired the songs in both *Maud* and *The Princess*, but the jingoism of the former repelled him, and his over-all impression of *The Princess* was touched with vague, indefinable disappointment. The poetic drama *Harold* he admired greatly, especially the last act.

Longfellow seems to have been greatly impressed by Browning's obscurity. "A wonderful man is Browning, but too obscure." He thought even *The Ring and the Book* obscure. It has been reported that upon being asked which of Browning's poems he liked best, he replied, "That which I understand best." Mrs. Browning, like most of his generation, he accepted more unquestioningly. The *Drama of Exile* was "very sublime and wonderful"; the *Sonnets from the Portuguese*, though perhaps too intimate, were "admirable"—"rather dusky at times, but deep and impassioned"; *Aurora Leigh* is "glorious," "deep, impassioned, strong, and tender."

Longfellow first encountered Matthew Arnold when Arthur Hugh Clough, visiting Cambridge, brought him a volume of Arnold's poems. He found them "very clever; with a little of the Tennysonian leaven in them." The next year there is a reference in his journal to Arnold's poems, "some of which I like." During his last visit to England he had a meeting with Dante Gabriel Rossetti, but according to Hall Caine, he supposed Rossetti the painter and Rossetti the poet to be two different men, so that upon taking leave of, as he supposed, the former, he left his regards for his brother, the poet, with special praise for "The Blessed Damozel."

What, now, of the less illustrious English poets, where the temptation to standardized reactions is not so strong? According to his sister Mrs. Pierce, the young Longfellow was very fond of Ossian, "which ... he used to read, and 'spout' a great deal," and later of *Lalla Rookh*. In 1874, after having not looked at Ossian for forty years, he took it up again and found that it still claimed some of its ancient power: "It is full of figures of the mist and rain that shroud the northern shores of Scotland and Ireland, and cannot be wholly a forgery."

He delighted in Cowley—"this half-forgotten, much-neglected bard"—and found Tom Taylor charming. Crabbe interested him when he encountered him in 1848, though he was painfully impressed by his sadness.

In his early life, he was fascinated by Chatterton and tried to get Jared Sparks to print an article about him in *The North American Review*. On the other hand, he disliked Blair's *The Grave* for its dwelling on the charnel-house aspects of death. The "well-rounded, ponderous periods" of Landor held "great charm" for him, and he found "wonderful dramatic power" in Beddoes. He thought Bailey's *Festus* wonderful in 1845 but could not read it at all in 1872. In 1847 he wrote Barry Cornwall that he found his lyrics "among the best in the language," and by 1852 they had become "almost the only real *songs* in the language." George Eliot's "The Legend of Jubal" exemplified for him the confusions of the "new style" in poetry, which he rejected, and in 1880 he hailed Frederick Locker-Lampson as "a power and a protest against the spirit and style that has of late years taken possession of a good deal of our poetry."

Among the eighteenth-century novelists, Defoe inspired some of Longfellow's earliest verses, and Sterne's influence seems reflected in the story of "The Little Man in Gosling Green." There is one admiring reference to Maria Edgeworth, but it concerns *The Parent's Assistant*, not the novels, and has clearly been influenced by memories of early years. I regret to report that he seems to have felt Jane Austen too detailed and matter-of-fact to appeal greatly to imaginative readers.

Lawrance Thompson has credited Scott with a large influence upon Longfellow, not only in diction and vocabulary but also in directing his attention to balladry and awakening his interest in European romance. Rereading *Marmion* after fifteen years in 1852, Longfellow was much impressed, especially by the last canto, which describes the Battle of Flodden Field. He was no less impressed with Scott's skill in describing battles when he reread *The Lady of the Lake* two years later, but now important non-aesthetic considerations were admitted also: "How much he has done to keep awake the war-spirit in England!" In 1860 he read in translation Ingemann's *Waldemar*, a Danish historical novel, "with the history rather too prominent to make a good Romance. But that is Ingemann's theory:—History in the foreground—Romance in the background:—just the reverse of Scott." A preference for Scott's method would seem to be implied.

In 1849 he enjoys the characterization in Bulwer-Lytton's novel, *The Caxtons*, but complains that "the style produces upon me the effect of a flashy waistcoat festooned with gold chains." But he seems to have been much more tolerant of a kindred vulgarity in Disraeli.

More important than any other novelist was Dickens, whom Longfellow admired for his genius and loved for his personal qualities. It required but one meeting, when the novelist first came to Boston in 1842, to convince Longfellow that Dickens was "a glorious fellow"—"a gay, free-and-easy character, with a fine bright face, blue eyes, and long dark hair, and withal a slight dash of the Dick Swiveller about him." Before the year was out, Dickens had royally entertained Longfellow in London. The letter Dickens wrote Longfellow from Broadstairs, September 28, 1842, fearing that he might have missed a visit through his absence from home, is in quite his liveliest vein, and the birthday letter he wrote him in Boston, on February 27, 1868, when he was too sick to keep a dinner engagement with him, must be one of the most charming letters of greeting that any man ever wrote or received.[9] This was, of course, during the novelist's second visit to America. Like the first meeting, this one promptly acquired an English sequel, and the whole Longfellow party was entertained at Gad's Hill in July 1868, which was the last time the two men saw each other.

Twenty-five years is a long stretch between two pairs of meetings, and correspondence seems to have done little or nothing to fill the gap. But, like all the rest of the world, the Longfellows read Dickens's writings diligently throughout the interval. Longfellow did not always admire. He accepted the strictures of *American Notes* with good grace, and it does not appear that his judgment of *Pictures of Italy* as "all drollery" while Goethe on the same subject was "all wisdom" was meant to be slighting, for he also calls the volume "the finest and funniest" book of travels he ever read. But he found *The Haunted Man* "rather tedious" and "The Wreck of the Golden Mary" much too tragic, and his comments on the various installments of the novels as they appeared are up-and-downish. *Chuzzlewit, Dombey,* and *Dorrit* drew the severest strictures, and he greatly admired *Copperfield, Bleak House,* and *Drood.* There is an interesting comment on *Pickwick,* made when he reread it in 1861: "It contains all Dickens in embryo, as an Overture does an Opera: themes and motives just touched upon which are more elaborately developed in later works."

Dickens is the only novelist who can be suspected of having influenced Longfellow's own writing. There is a good deal in *Kavanagh* quite in the spirit of Dickens whimsy: the description of Lucy and the baby at the beginning of Chapter II; the dismal clock in Chapter VIII—"gasping and catching its breath at times, and striking the hour with a violent, determined blow, reminding one of Jael driving the nail into the head of Sisera"; the poet H. Adolphus Hawkins, whose "shiny hair went off to the left in a superb sweep, like the handrail of a banister"; and the ardent lover who sends his inamorata "letters written with his own blood, —going barefooted into the brook to be bitten by leeches, and thus using his feet as inkstands." Quite like Dickens's animism, too, is the behavior of the little town at the beginning of "The Bell of Atri":

> One of those little places that have run
> Half up the hill, beneath a blazing sun,
> And then sat down to rest, as if to say,
> "I climb no farther upward, come what may."

The same note is struck in the journals. When he received the first proofs of *Evangeline* in the cheap edition of his poems, Longfellow wished that a wider measure might have been used:

It certainly would be a relief to the hexameters to let them stretch their legs a little more at their ease; still for the sake of uniformity I believe they must still sit a while longer with their knees bent under them like travellers in a stage-coach.

When, in 1858, the news of Dickens's separation from his wife came to hand, Longfellow was saddened:

What a sad affair is this of Dickens. Immensely exaggerated no doubt; but sad enough at best. How discouraging it is, and disgusting to see how eagerly and recklessly a fair reputation is dragged through the mire of the streets.[10]

But the tidings of June 1870 were much worse:

The terrible news from England [thus he writes John Forster], fills us all with inexpressible grief. Dickens was so full of life, that it did not seem possible he could die, and yet he has gone before us, and we are the mourners. I know what this loss will be to you, and cannot speak of it. I will not try to speak of it.

A week later he writes his brother Alexander, "Dickens is seldom out of my thoughts. He is a great loss to the world." But when he read Forster's *Life* the revelation contained in it of the novelist's driving restlessness during his last years overwhelmed Longfellow and oppressed him with melancholy: "It is a wonder that he lived so long."

Dickens's great rival Thackeray got off to a much less impressive start with the American poet, who found *Vanity Fair* "clever, but not very agreeable; and at the end tedious." *Esmond* fared better, as might have been expected, and so did both *The Newcomes* and *The Virginians*. By this time, Longfellow had met Thackeray and heard him lecture but had not been much taken with him. "He seems conceited and of the Grattan stamp." The Longfellows did not bother to attend Thackeray's last lecture in Boston, though it was given on a lovely day, but stayed home and read De Quincey instead.

Comments on the Brontës varied. *Villette* was judged "interesting" but "morbid," *Wuthering Heights* "fierce and wonderful," with "astonishing vigor of thought and style," all in all "a miracle." Mrs. Longfellow was very enthusiastic about *Shirley*, finding its "wonderfully vigorous and natural" style "a great improvement" over *Jane Eyre*. George Eliot's *Adam Bede* puzzled Longfellow, who thought it "too masculine for a woman, too feminine for a man," being in this less perspicacious than Dickens, who perceived at once that it must be woman's work. When Longfellow finally met George Eliot, he found her, as most people did, unexpectedly friendly and warm.

When Trollope visited Boston in 1861, both Longfellow and James T. Fields tried to catch up on their reading before greeting him. Like most readers of his time, Longfellow was much taken with Miss Mulock's *John Halifax, Gentleman*. There are a number of moderately favorable comments on Charles Reade, but no evidence that anything of Reade's ever took hold of Longfellow like Wilkie Collins's *Armadale*. When Charley lay wounded in Washington in Civil War days, his father read Miss Braddon's *Lady*

Audley's Secret to him, all through a long June day, and it made "the time pass swiftly and pleasantly."

In some memoranda she made for George Washington Greene in 1879, when he expected to write about Longfellow, Mrs. Pierce recalled her brother's early enjoyment of *The Spectator* and Johnson's *Lives of the Poets*. Later he himself calls Addison "musical and sweet," Steele "a little more sinewy . . . but far less charming." Pepys's *Diary* was "a droll book." Robert Stafford Ward sees in Burke an important influence upon him through awakening his appreciation of the emotive powers of language. Horace Walpole's letters were "always a remedy for a dull hour," and the seven volumes of Fanny Burney's diary helped him through the trying summer of 1862.

Longfellow also admired Landor's *Imaginary Conversations*, which he calls "strong and striking." In a conversation with Stanley Pumphrey, an English Friend, he took exception to Macaulay's treatment of William Penn. "The worst of it is, when a mistake was proved against him, Macaulay stuck to it; that is not worthy of a great mind." But the British nonfiction writer who draws the most comment is Carlyle. Longfellow was much impressed by *Sartor Resartus* and is reported to have called Carlyle "one of the few writers who have made history live." In 1838 he praised him for "his universal benevolence—the spirit of love in which he sees all men and all things," though he criticizes him for "the way he has of *ducking under* at the flash of every sharp-shooting inquiry." When he read the *Reminiscences*, however, he was not so sure of the benevolence.

Emerson and Hawthorne are the American writers whom Longfellow comes closest to considerately evaluating, but Irving and Bryant were the ones who had the largest influence upon him. The "pleasant humor," the "melancholy tenderness," and the "atmosphere of revery" in *The Sketch Book*—"even . . . its gray-brown covers, the shaded letters of its titles, and the fair clean type"—fascinated his imagination, excited and satisfied his mental hunger. Having discovered this work, he even began to see New England customs in the light of Irving's description of English customs. He imitated it in his projected New England sketch book, which Carey and Lea turned down, in the "Schoolmaster" papers, and above all in *Outre-Mer*, where the imitation extended even to format and method of publication. As for Bryant's important influence upon his early poetry, this was acknowledged by Longfellow himself and has been commented upon by many critics.

Longfellow seems to have encountered Emerson first as a lecturer; in this aspect he complains of his obscurity, *"dreamery,"* and lack of organization. In Emerson's lecture on "Great Men" he found "many things to shock the sensitive ear and heart," but a few days later, having heard him on Goethe, he calls him "the Chrysostom and Sir Thomas Browne of the day." They had tea together on February 4, 1846, and enjoyed a pleasant meeting. But Emerson's lectures continued to draw mixed notices from the Craigie House. In 1849 Longfellow found his discourse on inspiration itself inspired, but two years later he "had not the most remote idea" what the Concord sage was "driving at" when he held forth on fate. In April 1854 he heard him read his lecture on poetry in such "a very nonchalant and careless manner" that though the lecture itself was "full of brilliant and odd things," it was "not very satisfactory" to listen to.[11]

When the *Essays* first appeared in 1841, Longfellow reported to his father:

In literature there is nothing new, save Mr. Emerson's Essays, which have just appeared; full of sublime prose-poetry, magnificent absurdities, and simple truths. It is a striking book; but as it is impossible to see any connection in the ideas, I do not think it would please you much, and I shall not send it.

His comment on the *Poems,* in his journal, five years later, is similarly discriminating, though not unappreciative:

It gave us the keenest pleasure, though many of the pieces present themselves Sphinx-like, and "struggling to get free their hinder-parts," present a very bold front and challenge your answer. Throughout the volume, through the golden mist and sublimation of fancy gleam bright veins of purest poetry, like rivers running through meadows. Truly a rare volume! With many exquisite poems in it, among which I should single out "Monadnoc," "Threnody," "The Humble-bee," as containing much of the quintessence of poetry.

Basically, Longfellow's difficulty with Emerson was his own "early Unitarian" outlook. The later development of Transcendentalism largely passed him by. In the first number of *The Dial* he found "affectation," "beauty," "wisdom and folly"—all in all, "a strange mixture." He read *Walden* but he had nothing of consequence to say about it, and neither he nor Mrs. Longfellow ever had much sympathy for the Alcotts. Yet his specific criticisms are generally just, and on at least one occasion contact with Emerson robbed him of respect for his own work:

I heard Emerson last evening on Plato—a most curious cluster of fancies and philosophies sometimes deep and most suggestive, then wild, vague, and unsatisfactory, but expressed with a beauty which ravished me. As I listened, I thought of the lotus-eaters. After him I feel almost a nausea at all that I can do—at my scarlet, green-burze, holyoke-flower stuff.

Hawthorne Longfellow early appreciated with complete adequacy, as his appreciative paper on *Twice-Told Tales* attests. His personal contacts with Hawthorne were consistently pleasant also. "He is a strange owl; a very peculiar individual, with a dash of originality about him very pleasant to behold." He was delighted with "The Birthmark," thinking that "the comet himself" could not "unfold a more glorious *tail*," and only complaining that the author had not developed it into a romance instead of stopping with a short story.[12] Longfellow himself got the story of *Evangeline* from Hawthorne and was always grateful for it. He praised *The Scarlet Letter* as standing "pre-eminent among works of American fiction." In *The House of the Seven Gables* he found not "more power" but "a greater diversity of power." When *The Marble Faun* arrived, he broke his rule against night reading for it, "almost putting out" his eyes while Fanny and Charley went to hear Mrs. Kemble read *Hamlet*.

In his youth, Longfellow was attracted by Brockden Brown's *Arthur Mervyn,* but he seems more inspired by patriotism here than by purely literary considerations. He seems not to have owned a set of Cooper until 1856. Then he read *The Two Admirals,* and though he found the style old-fashioned, he gave the author credit for "strength and determination and self-reliance" and for leaving "an impression of greatness on the reader's mind." But a few months later he did not enjoy *Homeward Bound* and *Home As Found* at all.

He read *Typee* in the summer of 1846 and found it "very curious and interesting," though Mrs. Longfellow seems to have been shocked by Fayaway. He was delighted with Melville's anonymous article on Hawthorne's *Mosses,* of which he sent Hawthorne a copy, and on November 15, 1851, he read *Moby-Dick* all evening and found it "very wild, strange and interesting." But there is no follow-up; neither did he comment on any of Melville's later works.[13]

In the only letter he ever wrote to Poe, Longfellow told him that "all I have read from your pen has inspired me with a high idea of your power, and I think you are destined to stand among the first romance-writers of the country, if such be your aim." He liked Robert Montgomery Bird personally but could not "stand" his books. His respect for N. P. Willis declined after personal contact and along with it his interest in his writings. He objected only to the power of *Uncle Tom's Cabin,* which was "too melancholy" and made his "blood boil too hotly." He thought that J. H. Ingraham, who dedicated *Pirate of the Gulf* to him—"but without permission, confound him"—wrote "the worst novels ever written by anybody," yet when *The Prince of the House of David* appeared, he could not but find some merit in it. He discerned "poetic genius" in Sylvester Judd's *Richard Edney* but was distressed by its structural deficiencies.

Among the works of the younger novelists, he is said to have admired Cable's *The Grandissimes* and to have hoped that it might typify a new style in fiction. He also praised Elizabeth Stuart

Phelps, especially for *The Story of Avis*—"the most beautiful analysis of a noble woman's nature that I have seen in any work of fiction." In 1874 he congratulated Howells on the current installment of *A Foregone Conclusion* in the *Atlantic*.

He encouraged the younger poets in his later years also—Lanier, Aldrich, Gilder, Hayne, and others—but his insistence upon simplicity of style made him cold to the experimentalists.[14] He was kind to Whitman personally, and if he was less responsive to his poetry than Emerson was, he was certainly much more so than Lowell or Whittier. In 1873 Julia Ward Howe's *Passion Flowers* pleased him by its "genius" and "beauty" but distressed him by its sadness and "discontent." "Here is revolt enough between these blue covers." [15]

Longfellow read extensively in a number of European literatures —sometimes in the original and sometimes in translation. His long preoccupation with Dante gave the Italian a special importance for him. When he resumed his interrupted translation of the "Purgatorio" in 1853, he declared that it "diffused its benediction through the day." Michael Angelo is permitted to enter rather severe judgments of both Petrarch and Ariosto, which Longfellow must in some measure have shared. The poet can be severe, also, on Goldoni, Ariosto, and Boccaccio, but he knew how to relish them as well. In *Tales of a Wayside Inn*, Boccaccio, despite his sensuality, is both praised and drawn upon:

> The story-telling bard of prose,
> Who wrote the joyous Tuscan tales
> Of the Decameron, that make
> Fiesole's green hills and vales
> Remembered for Boccaccio's sake.

For Calderón and Lope de Vega, Longfellow seems to have had much the same kind of feeling that he had for these Italians. He was not willing to go along with the German critics in sacrificing Lope to Calderón. He admits that Calderón has more imagination and a more poetical style, but he finds his diction pompous. Lope, though careless, has more force, simplicity, and directness. Yet when, under the stress of the Civil War, Longfellow sought relief in literature, it was to Calderón that he turned.

Victor Hugo is probably the French writer he praises most, but George Sand is the one to whom he refers most often. It is true that she gets only a qualified endorsement, the reservations being entered, as might have been expected, upon moral grounds. Carl Johnson, who found references to fifteen George Sand titles in Longfellow, could not find that he spoke of her at all after 1860. Nevertheless, as he remarks, she had held the poet's interest for twenty years longer than Mlle de Scudéry, Mme de Sévigne, or Mme de Pompadour, each of whom had fascinated him for a time.

A number of other French novelists are mentioned however. In 1848 he read Balzac's *Scènes de la vie de province*. "He has wonderful skill in the delineation of characters; but over all his tales is 'the trail of the serpent.' " In spite of this, however, Higginson remembered that he commended *La Peau de chagrin* to his students as a model of style. In his lecture notes on Balzac he calls *Père Goriot* "a King Lear in low life" and describes Josephine as "one of the most striking characters ever drawn by the pen of a romancer." The same lecture contains notes on a number of works by a nineteenth-century French novelist often considered shocking, Paul de Kock. *Georgette* is condemned for its "lewdness" and *Gustave* for its "indecency and licentiousness," but *Le Bon Enfant* gets a clean bill of health.

In 1858 he calls *The Three Musketeers* amusing, but the very next year *The Count of Monte Cristo* is "very clever in construction, but spun out beyond everything." Stendhal's *La Chartreuse de Parme* is "a bad book," "a clever description of Italian manners," which "grows worse and worse" as it proceeds. Erckmann-Chatrian's *Le Blocus* gets a sympathetic hearing, possibly because Longfellow sympathized with its pacifism. There are several references to that Gallicized Russian, Turgenev, generally favorable, though one unnamed book is described as painful. He read *The Wandering Jew* by Eugène Sue and wrote some nonsense verses inspired by its great length. At the end of his life—in 1880—he told Amy Fay that he had never read a novel by Zola.

Among the older French writers, Rabelais "wearies" him in 1874. Molière he appreciated, with some reservations. In 1850 Racine's *Athalie* prompts a generalization: "What a strange world is this of the old French drama! Not unnatural, but supernatural. One must step up onto the platform!" In his lecture on "The Trouvères" he is very apologetic about the fabliaux, but perhaps no more so than the times demanded. A visit to Ferney in 1836 had already prompted a slighting reference to Voltaire: "I have no regard nor respect for the memory of this evil spirit whose countenance was 'half eagle half monkey'—and whose mind partook of the character of his countenance."

Longfellow praised Chateaubriand's glowing descriptions of American scenery and condemned Lamartine's "long-winded raptures." In the 'seventies he found Taine's history of English literature "a prodigiously clever book." He recommended Sainte-Beuve very highly to his son Charley, calling *Causeries de lundi* and *Nouveaux Lundis* "charmingly written essays on various subjects historical, literary and artistic."

Except for Dante's work in Italian, German literature was more important to Longfellow than that of any other continental nation, and he found comfort in Novalis and other romanticists after Mary's death. Yet his approach to the giant of German literature was cautious in the extreme. In the beginning he greatly preferred both Schiller and Jean-Paul Richter.

His enthusiasm for Schiller was fired by Carlyle, and his early inclination to prefer him to Goethe was determined not only by Schiller's more idealistic moral atmosphere but also by Longfellow's own conviction that the poet should be close to the heart of humanity, writing not only for "the few who think" but also for "the many who feel."

Longfellow praises Richter in his manuscript lectures on German literature and in the rhapsodic chapter about him in *Hyperion*. He admires Richter for the goodness of his heart and the purity of his life, his "boundless love for all that is good in man and all that is beautiful in the world," and his "magnificent and gorgeous imagination, which makes his descriptions of nature like Claude Lorrain's sunset landscapes." But he is under no delusions concerning the German's ability to please English and American readers in general. Like Sterne, he is a lawless genius who insists upon going his own way, and the reader must accept him upon his own terms.

Longfellow also appreciated Heine's lyrical gift, but he had nothing in common with his spirit. The severest indictment is to be found in an 1842 article in *Graham's Magazine*, where Heine appears as "the leader of the new school in Germany which is seeking to establish a religion of sensuality, and to build a palace of Pleasure on the ruins of the church." He is "not sufficiently in earnest to be a great poet." As late as 1864 Longfellow finds Heine's recent verses, written after his illness, "witty and wicked as ever."

Longfellow praises Lessing's *Nathan the Wise:* "I think highly of it;—though it is not a masterpiece; and I do not like the way in which it closes. The story of the Three Rings, told by Nathan the Jew—is beautiful, and as good as a sermon." *Emilia Galotti*, on the other hand, is called "a horrible tragedy," and *Miss Sara Sampson* is "still less pleasing. . . . Why choose such a theme?"

Longfellow's relationship to Goethe is a very large subject which has now been studied in detail by other writers [16] and which, therefore, need only be viewed in its broadest outlines here. In the beginning *The Sorrows of Werther* fascinated him by its sweet simplicity, reminiscent of Wordsworth, yet too naked and natural for English readers, while at the same time it repelled him by its unhealthy emotionalism, eventuating in suicide, and its lack of Christian principle. Even *Faust* was recommended only for "healthy, manly, and strong minds, for moral fire-eaters, who have an antidote for Prussic acid." The original title for the Goethe chapter in *Hyperion* was "Old Humbug." In 1851 he advised Roelker not to publish an English translation of the *Elective Affinities,* and it was not until 1871 that Goethe's portrait replaced

Schiller's as the frontispiece of *The Poets and Poetry of Europe*. On the other hand, Longfellow found himself defending Goethe against Menzel's attack upon him as early as 1840, for he was already perceiving how, with all his shortcomings, Goethe had at last "perfected himself" from "a buoyant, cloudless youth" into "a free, benignant, lofty-minded man," finally achieving a "classic repose." For all his half-heartedness in the matter, Longfellow rendered great service to the Goethe cause in the United States. It was he who delivered the first lectures on Gothe ever heard at Harvard. As Orie W. Long puts it, he was "the first important interpreter in this country of . . . [Goethe's] genius and fame."

III

Since Longfellow was, for much of his life, a professional scholar and teacher, he made a more direct use of his knowledge than he would have made if he had been exclusively a creative writer. Of the quality of his mind, and of his scholarship in general, various estimates have been made. As early as 1834, George Ticknor thought "his knowledge of the language and literature" of France, Italy, and Spain "quite extraordinary."

He writes and speaks Spanish with a degree of fluency and exactness, which I have known in no other American born of Parents speaking the English as their vernacular. His knowledge of Spanish Literature is extensive and to be relied upon; and several publications he has made on the subject, have been accompanied with poetical translations of much spirit and fidelity. Besides this, he is, for his years, an accomplished general scholar, particularly in modern literature; and full of activity and eagerness in the pursuit of knowledge.[17]

His early biographer, George Rice Carpenter, on the other hand, was never willing to credit him with more than "care, industry, and good taste. Unexcelled as a translator, he had not caught the new and powerful spirit of organized research, or even of criticism based on other grounds than personal preference," and more recent judgments have ranged from Lawrance Thompson's somewhat contemptuous view, through Andrew Hilen's rather severe evaluation of his achievements in the Scandinavian field, to the more generous assessments of Hatfield, Goggio, Miss Whitman, and Stanley T. Williams.[18]

I do not wish to suggest that these scholars never approach a meeting of minds. Hatfield does not claim that Longfellow became "a towering specialist" of the Ticknor variety. Goggio admits that his indifference to—and virtual denial of—the allegorical element in *The Divine Comedy* prevented him from bringing out "the full significance of Dante's work." Hilen, on the other hand, finds that his translations from the Scandinavian, "although few in number, are among the most successful in the language," and even Thompson sees his scholastic achievements as considerable during the time of the Bowdoin professorship, when he was giving his full time to scholarship.

That Longfellow had a gift for language study has never been seriously questioned. On his first trip to Europe, writes Carl Johnson, "he learned to speak French, Spanish, and Italian, and made himself familiar with German." On the second, "he perfected his knowledge of German, and learned how to read Finnish, Swedish, Danish, Norwegian, and Dutch. He also acquainted himself with Portuguese and Provençal." Moreover, he "had no easy texts with carefully prepared vocabularies and notes. He had to dig out the meaning of each sentence with the aid of a dictionary. Reading French was rather like translating Latin."

He never pretended that progress was easy or automatic. "If I had known before leaving home how hard a task I was undertaking," he writes his father in 1826, "I should have shrunk." And, more fully, the next year:

Do not believe what people tell you of learning the French language in six months and the Spanish in three. Were I guided by such counsellors I should return a sheer charlatan; and though I might deceive others as to the amount of my knowledge, I cannot so easily deceive myself.

Yet the summary of his achievements which he sent home at the end of 1828 is not contemptible:

With the French and Spanish languages I am familiarly conversant, so as to speak them correctly, and write them with as much ease and fluency as I do the English. The Portuguese I read without difficulty. And with regard to my proficiency in the Italian, I have only to say that all at the hotel where I lodge took me for an Italian until I told them I was an American.

In Germany the difficulties were multiplied, for he found German an unbelievably difficult language, "not to read—that is not so hard—but to write." By 1833 he was translating from the German and buying German books for the Bowdoin library. During his second visit to Europe his interest in German was much keener, and in *Hyperion* the lady who tells Paul Flemming that she cannot endure the German harshness is bluntly informed that she would like it better if she were more familiar with it. "It is not harsh to me, but homelike, hearty, and full of feeling—like the sound of happy voices at a fireside, of a winter's night, when the wind blows, and the fire crackles, and hisses, and snaps." By 1837, in a letter to Mary Appleton, Longfellow found German a better language than English in which to express his feelings for her sister Fanny.

He began his Swedish and Finnish in Stockholm in 1835. The Swedish at least he found "slow work. It comes word by word, and phrase by phrase." But it did come, and it got far enough so that he was able to contribute a discussion of the Dalecarlian dialect to Bosworth's *Dictionary of the Anglo-Saxon Language* in 1838. One September day in 1835, at Copenhagen, he took his first Icelandic lesson in the morning and his first Danish lesson in the afternoon. He did not like Danish at first. "For softness and beauty it cannot be compared with the beautiful Swedish. The Danes speak with a *burr* in their throats which cannot be defined." But within a few days he is translating Danish poems and reading an early Danish comedy. Dutch too he mastered, sufficiently for conversational purposes, within a month.

Hilen disposes of Longfellow's knowledge of the literary history of Norway in one footnote, saying merely that he knew very little about it. In Danish literature he was concerned most with the old ballads, though he was not ignorant of important contemporary figures. Andersen he seems to have been content to read in translation. "Like many of Andersen's admirers ... he overlooked the irony, the social import, and the deep seriousness of his work: he understood him only as a writer of fairy tales and as a man of charming imagination." Late in life, when Longfellow was appealed to by Henry Johnson as a kind of authority on Icelandic literature, he disclaimed knowledge of anything more than the *Heimskringla* and a few other pieces and professed only "the most elementary knowledge" of Old Norse.

Longfellow's rapid progress in his language studies was furthered by two considerations. In the first place, he brought imagination as well as industry to his study. "I like to read dictionaries. Some words have a perfume about them like flowers. Others are quaint and pleasing to the eye, like the fantastic gables of an old house." He also had complete faith in the importance of language study and great enthusiasm for it. In March 1828 he writes his mother from Rome that he is "completely enchanted" with the study of languages and "passionately fond of it." By autumn he is trying to draw his sisters into the charmed circle: "I assure you that, by every language you learn, a new world is opened before you. It is like being born again; and new ideas break upon the mind with all the freshness and delight with which we may suppose the first dawn of intellect to be accompanied." Four years later, in an article in *The North American Review*, Longfellow stated his views on the importance of language study to all the world:

We hold the study of languages, philosophically pursued, to be one of the most important which can occupy the human mind. And we are borne out in this opinion, by the reflection, that the elements of language lie deep among the elements of thought:—that the one follows the various fluctuations of the other; and that the language of a nation is the external symbol of its character and its mind.[19]

Longfellow's intellectual life was not, however, entirely limited to his areas of specialization. When, in 1824, he was trying to reconcile his father to the idea of a literary career, he both claimed "a most voracious appetite for knowledge" and reproached himself for not having hitherto seized upon his opportunities with sufficient zeal. It does not appear that his neglect can have been very culpable at any period. He graduated from Bowdoin fourth in a class of thirty-eight and delivered an English Oration at the Commencement exercises. Even his elementary school teachers had been pleased with him, and we are told that he was halfway through the Latin grammar at seven, standing above "several boys twice as old as he." It is true that he had no love for mathematics; neither was he a naturally good speller.[20] He is also reported to have disliked forensics and to have been indifferent to "the mere bare facts of Mental Science; I loved them clothed in appropriate words."

Natural science he did not care much for either—though one of his best teachers at Bowdoin was Parker Cleaveland, and later Louis Agassiz was one of his best friends. He was always greatly interested in the weather, but that was purely a practical interest, and only once did he even pretend to analyze the scientific phenomena involved. Intellectually he agrees with Agassiz that science ought to be an inspiration for poetry, even epic poetry, but he insists that he is not the man for the job. Occasionally he reads a scientific book or attends a scientific lecture or demonstration. He may even take a scientific illustration for a poem. One of these, in "The Two Angels," seems very Tennysonian:

> And my soul sank within me, as in wells
> The waters sink before an earthquake's shock.

Once, too, science suggests a title to him: "The Occultation of Orion." Essentially, however, what he wants from science is romantic and spiritual suggestiveness. When he hears Dr. Nichols lecture on the moon, he thinks that "many maidens must be *désillusionnées,* finding the soft planet changed to vast barren rocks, without cloud, without water, without atmosphere, without inhabitant." If so, the "maidens" were not alone in their disillusionment.

What a wide sweep the subject has; and how poetical! [This is Long-fellow after hearing a lecture by a distinguished botanist.] Among other things he told us that the Greeks brought the vine into Europe; the Roman armies, wheat and cherries; and the Arabs, the orange and the olive. In a triumphal entry of Lucullus into Rome, a cherry-tree in full bearing was carried in the procession.

But the interest here is clearly centered not in science but in the romance of history.

In the tribute Longfellow sent to Agassiz on his fiftieth birthday he spoke of the natural world as "the manuscripts of God," and that was the way he really liked to think about it. When he looks through Dr. Nichols's telescope he forgets his body altogether: "The soul seems to assert its supremacy and to walk among the stars." Again, he wishes that he had a mind "so well balanced, and swinging on such noiseless hinges" as a great telescope. All in all, perhaps science came closest to giving Longfellow an intellectual thrill when he felt his faith strengthened by it. Thus he looks through a microscope and cries to Oliver Wendell Holmes: "Credo quia impossibile est." And he adds, "I will never hereafter doubt the impossible possibilities of the unseen. These revelations of the microscope are perfectly astounding."

Philosophy was another matter altogether. Paul Flemming of *Hyperion* expresses impatience with philosophical and theological speculation, but the Professor assures him that he will be wiser about these things when he is older. Longfellow himself read Locke as early as 1823, finding him both more interesting and less difficult than he had expected. In 1830 he guided a Bowdoin student through a course of reading in Cousin, Degerando, and Constant. In 1846 he read Fichte, apparently expecting to be shocked by him. Instead he found "more of the soul of Christian-ity in these lectures than in the sermons of all the rebel crew of narrow-minded, dyspeptic, so-called *orthodox* preachers who rail against German philosophy."

Robert Stafford Ward has given more attention to Longfellow's interest in philosophy than his other critics, finding in him a characteristic adherence to "that peculiarly American product, pragmatic idealism." Longfellow dismissed metaphysical speculation as beyond the range of the human understanding and rejected salvation through faith without works. He opposed utilitarianism. His attitude toward the immortality of the soul was influenced by his study of the law of the conservation of energy. Ward says:

In *The Poets and Poetry of Europe*, the account of Herder gives him credit for "his great picture of the progress of the world"; and though Longfellow did not himself write all of the historical accounts in the volume, he certainly approved of all that was said in them. In Sumner's famous oration—"The Law of Human Progress"—he traced the German origins of the doctrine back through Herder to the Italian, Vico. Longfellow shared most of Sumner's views, and Sumner had sought the aid of George W. Greene in preparing the historical data for his address. The German scholar, Schulze, has recognized the influence. And, finally, the philosophical background of such works as "The Occultation of Orion," "The Saga of King Olaf," "The Building of the Ship," *Hiawatha*, and *Christus* fits perfectly into Herder's version of Vico's cyclical theory of history. Whether derived from Herder directly or indirectly, or both, the theory certainly was a part of Longfellow's philosophy of life; and no thorough understanding of his work is possible without reference to it.

IV

Longfellow's ideal as a teacher was a lofty one. He stated it in his Inaugural Address at Bowdoin:

I regard the profession of teacher in a far more noble and elevated point of view than many do. I cannot help believing that he who bends in a right direction the pliant disposition of the young, and trains up the ductile mind to a vigorous and healthy growth, does something for the welfare of his country and something for the great interests of humanity.

He was a diligent teacher, too, and, as we have seen, when he found no textbooks ready to his hand, he proceeded to prepare them himself, basing them upon the principle, then too little recognized, that education cannot be successful unless it enlists the interest of the pupil. Moreover, he was an important and influential one, for he made a very large contribution toward establishing the study of the modern languages as a basic part of American education. Speaking of Longfellow and Ticknor together, Professor Johnson says of this aspect:

They gave the first advanced instruction in the modern languages. They opened the fields of modern literature and were the first language teachers to provide work above the level of basic grammar and elementary reading. It was a liberal, progressive step. As a result, the Department of Modern Languages at Harvard offered the first advanced training in modern literature. This pioneer work led naturally to the development of graduate study.

Longfellow always prepared his lectures in a responsible manner, sometimes expending "the labor of weeks" upon a single discourse. The examination of his unpublished notes and manuscripts leaves me with the feeling that while he achieved less in the way of a blanket coverage of his subject than would be expected today, he took more of his materials from first-hand sources in a number of languages than most contemporary professors do. He attempted little critical analysis and was much given to the reading of specimens which permitted the writer under consideration to speak for himself. This was a self-effacing way, and it might easily be defended as sound pedagogic procedure in a period when many of the texts were difficult or impossible for students to come by at first hand.

Among Longfellow's books there is an 1831 edition of *Faust* which he had bound up with blank leaves for memoranda, and from which he taught. Some of his notes are explications of the text, but more are quotations from a wide range of authors whom Goethe's work in some way recalls or resembles. In making such a commentary, with its abundance of comparisons and illustrations, Longfellow was following Ticknor's own method, as advocated in his 1832 lecture on the best methods of teaching the living languages.

At the same time, Longfellow understood what we call the

historical method, as we may see by these remarks from his lecture on Molière:

However great a man may be, he never stands entirely alone. He is always one of a group. This one did him such and such a favor; that one, such and such an injury; and he married the aunt or sister of a third, and was thus operated upon by new influences. I need not tell you, that apparently trivial circumstances often change a man's whole life. Hence when we speak of an individual we have likewise to speak of the age in which he lived. You disguise a portrait if you cut it out of its frame. You disfigure a character if you cut it out of its "environment."

Though this sounds deceptively simple, the scholarly notions involved are basic. Indeed, its simplicity recalls Saintsbury's penetrating remark that he is never sure whether Longfellow really did not go very deeply into anything or only seemed not to. Much Longfellow criticism has been vitiated by failure to observe this distinction.

Of course this does not mean that everybody liked Longfellow as a teacher. Edward Everett Hale, for example, found the first lecture on *Faust* "very flowery and bombastical indeed, which appeared to me very much out of taste." The future author of *The Man Without a Country* liked the second lecture better, but he did not attend any sessions not required of him. Yet when the professor met his class in the Corporation Room, around a mahogany table, "the whole affair had the aspect of a friendly gathering in a private house, in which the study of German was the amusement of the occasion."

A more enthusiastic reaction to Longfellow's teaching was registered by Daniel R. Goodwin, one of his first pupils at Bowdoin:

To a musical voice and singularly facile organs, to a refined taste, a ready command of the best English, and a thorough acquaintance with the language and literature he taught—he added an affable and winning manner, a warmth of enthusiasm, a magnetic power, a ready sympathy and an inexhaustible patience, which made his lecture-room and the studies of his department a joy and a pleasure at the time, and ever afterwards a happy memory.

Yet Longfellow did not enjoy teaching. To be sure, there were times when he thought he did. "I have finished my lectures for this term; and am very busy preparing for next Spring and Summer. It is delightful. I have a great deal of time at my command; and make pretty good use of it." Again, he finds himself "in very good spirits; and care[s] not that the vacation is over." It is gratifying, too, when the "boys" appear "gloriously" in an examination, "so that Prescott and the rest of the Committee said they had never attended so good an examination."

But for every such expression of satisfaction there are many expressions of impatience. "It seems like folly to record the college days—the working in the crypts of life, the underground labor. Pardon me, O ye who, seeing education only from afar, speak of it in such glowing words!" Examinations in particular are "anguish and exhaustion." But the bondage is worse than the labor. "It is not the labor, but the being bound hand and foot, the going round and round in a tread-mill, that oppresses me." All in all, it is "a dog's life," and he looks forward eagerly to retirement long before he finally brings it about.

It is also true, to be sure, that he is more slow and hesitant about making the final break than might have been expected of a man with his means and resources, and when at last he achieves it, he cannot deny that "there is a good deal of sadness in the feeling of separating one's self from one's former life." But the last commencement he attended seemed to him "ghostly and unreal, as a thing in which I had no part." "My reason for leaving the College," he tells his sister Anne, "is in part the helpless state of my eyes; and in part the weariness of doing the same things over and over again for so many, many years."

Yet it is clear all the time that what he dislikes is not so much the teaching in itself as the fact that it keeps getting in the way of what he wants to do much more. "The college work is like a great hand laid on all the strings of my lyre, stopping their vibrations." "I mean to turn author," he writes from Bowdoin in 1832, "and write a book—not a *grammar*." In 1846, at Harvard, the note is the same. If he is going to be a writer, then he ought to give all his energy to writing. "I am a fool and a madman to lead the life I do." He admits that if he were willing to give all his time to his college duties, things would work out quite comfortably, but he cannot bring himself to do this, with "such an ardent temper as mine." And so even that which he might otherwise have enjoyed became a new source of discomfort: "Today a new class in college wanting to read Faust. And I cannot in conscience say No.... It is only one more impediment between me and the real work I have to do."

One aspect of Longfellow's dissatisfaction with teaching was that he got very tired of "hearing great themes discussed by boys," and of making his own mind "constantly a playmate for boys—constantly adapting itself to them, instead of stretching out and grappling with *men's* minds." He might have relished this aspect of his work more if he had enjoyed dominating people, but there was nothing of that form of sadism in him—nor, indeed, of any other.

Longfellow's relations with his students were courteous but not intimate. He "did not cultivate us much personally," says Higginson, "or ask us to his house, but he remembered and acknowledged our salutations. He was, I think, the first Harvard instructor who addressed the individual student with the prefix 'Mr.' " "His intercourse with the students was perfectly simple, frank, and manly," wrote one who himself afterwards became a college president. "He neither sought popularity nor repelled it." For the maintenance of order and discipline he relied more upon the dignity of his presence and the interest with which he presented his materials than upon any of the more obvious disciplinary resources generally in vogue in a day when college students in general were much younger than they are today. When a rebuke had to be given, he was never inconsiderate or cruel, and he understood the relief of humor, not only to alleviate the sting of the rebuke but to fix it in memory. Suggestions are not lacking that some of the boys would have found a more approachable, rough-and-ready manner easier to take, even if it had been coupled with less perfect courtesy, yet we are told that when they were involved in a college riot, they would listen only to him among the faculty members because, as they put it, he always treated them like gentlemen—which, incidentally, is just what, in this connection, they were not.

Whether the yoke galled him more at Harvard or at Bowdoin it would be hard to say. Conditions were worse at Bowdoin. In 1830 he sent his friend George Washington Greene this account of his daily schedule:

I rise at six in the morning, and hear a French recitation of sophomores immediately. At seven I breakfast, and am then master of my time until eleven, when I hear a Spanish lesson of Juniors. After that I take lunch; and at twelve I go into the library, where I remain till one. I am then at leisure for the afternoon till five, when I have a French recitation of Juniors. At six, I take coffee; then walk and visit friends till nine; study till twelve, and sleep till six, when I begin the same round again.

But he was younger when he did this than he was to be at Harvard, and he was asking less of himself and of life. For one thing, he was not trying to practice his art:

Since my return, I have written one piece of poetry, but I have not published a line....I am all prudence now, since I can form a more accurate judgment of the merit of poetry. If I ever publish a volume, it will be many years first. Indeed, I have such an engrossing interest in the studies of my profession that I write very seldom except in connection with those studies.

But there were other circumstances at Bowdoin which made Longfellow very uncomfortable. The college was in about as disorganized a state as a college can be if it is to continue to function. Moreover, Longfellow's liberal religious views made him an object of suspicion, and in some quarters the feeling against him seems to have been keen.

The attempt which the college had made, while he was in Europe, to substitute an instructorship for a professorship had made Longfellow about as angry as anything that ever happened to him. As he wrote his father from Göttingen:

... with regard to Bowdoin College, the more I think of it, the more I am dissatisfied. So much so, indeed, that I am adverse to going there at all, if any other situation can be procured me. I dislike the manner in which things are conducted there. Their illiberality in point of religion—and their narrow-minded views upon many other points, need no comment. Had I the means of a bare subsistence, I would *now* refuse a Professorship there. I say *now:* I mean since they had offered me a lower office.

He refused the lower office, as we have seen, and the offer of the professorship was renewed and accepted, but he would not have been human if the clash had left no scars.

Finally, the young professor who came to Bowdoin was not the same man—or boy—who had been delighted, upon his graduation, to receive an offer there. He had spent three years in Europe meanwhile and acquired a new cosmopolitanism of outlook.

I have aimed higher than this [he writes his sister Annie in 1831]: and I cannot believe that all my aspirations are to terminate in the drudgery of a situation which gives me no opportunity to distinguish myself, and in point of worldly gain, does not even pay me for my labor. Besides, one loses ground so fast in these out of the way places: the mind has no stimulus to exertion—grows sluggish in its movements and narrow in its sphere—and there's the end of a man. We will see.

Longfellow's remaining at Bowdoin as long as he did was not due to any lack of reasonable—or even unreasonable—efforts to get away. He flirted with New York University and the University of Virginia. He cast longing glances toward an editorship or a diplomatic post. Against his wife's advice, he made a journey of inspection to George Bancroft's Round Hill School for boys, at Northampton, Massachusetts; he also pondered the possibility of establishing an independent girls' school in New York.[21] Once he even contemplated burning his bridges behind him and going to Manhattan without assurances to make his way in journalism! And when he revisited Brunswick, several years after having left it, he wrote George Hillard that he "would not for all the world live again in that little world—so 'remote, unfriended, melancholy, slow.' "

When the Harvard offer came in 1834, it seemed a happy solution of all his problems. He had been casting longing eyes toward the Athens on the Charles for some time. But even in Paradise, he was to learn, the grass looks greener from outside the gate. His work itself was far from easy.

I am working pretty hard at college. I have three lectures a week, and recitations without number. Three days in the week I go into my class-room between seven and eight, and come out between three and four—with one hour's intermission. The other days are consumed in preparation, and in doing the usual small matters which every man has to do, with the usual interruptions.

As chairman of a department, Longfellow had the supervision of the foreign instructors under him—"this *four-in-hand* of outlandish animals, all pulling the wrong way, except one,—this gives me more trouble than anything else. I have more anxiety about their doing well than about my own. I think I should be more satisfied if I did all the work myself." Sometimes they did not do their work, or did it badly. Two, at least, had to be asked to resign. And sometimes the college itself did not, in his opinion, treat them fairly, and then he would find himself involved with the administration in their behalf. Much as he hated strife, he never dodged an issue, but he did not always win. His difficulties were increased by the fact that his department was not one of the most firmly established in the college. In many quarters, it was regarded, rather, as an upstart department, and rested, consequently, under the perpetual necessity of fighting for its place.

Even in relation to university affairs as a whole, Longfellow often found himself opposed to his colleagues and superiors. He disliked public academic exercises, and he was very impatient of all academic red tape. And though he had no interest in administration as such, he did have convictions about education. He believed in the elective system, for example, and his outlook in general was what in his time must have been considered distinctly forward-looking.

It is not surprising, therefore, that once he had got settled at

Harvard, Longfellow should have found himself scarcely more contented there than he had been at Bowdoin. Once he found himself suggesting a reduction in his already inadequate stipend in order to shed unwelcome administrative duties. Once, at least, the old diplomatic dream revived. And once he even contemplated a fantastic piece of rashness. For if we find it difficult to envision Longfellow as a free-lancing New York journalist, what *are* we to say of a Longfellow who considered resigning his professorship to go to Europe as tutor and guide to a young scion of the house of Astor? Yet he seriously applied for this post in 1839, and it was not his wisdom but the elder Astor's vacillation, plus the scrupulous care of Longfellow's own guardian angel, that saved him from it.

CHAPTER FOUR

"Art is long and Time is fleeting"

I

Never much given to the formulation of dogma in any area, Longfellow would not seem to have framed any very elaborate poetic theory, and, quite naturally, an age which is more interested in poetic theory than in poetry has made him pay for this. Almost his only widely read utterance on the subject is in what seems a very simple poem, "The Day Is Done"; one wonders why so few persons seem able to understand it. This is the poem in which the poet turns away, for the moment, from the "grand old masters" and

> the bards sublime
> Whose distant footsteps echo
>   Through the corridors of Time.
>
> For, like strains of martial music,
>   Their mighty thoughts suggest
> Life's endless toil and endeavor;
>   And tonight I long for rest.
>
> Read from some humbler poet,
>   Whose songs gushed from his heart,
> As showers from the clouds of summer,
>   Or tears from the eyelids start.

The poem ends with some of Longfellow's best-known lines:

> Then read from the treasured volume
> The poem of thy choice,
> And lend to the rhyme of the poet
> The beauty of thy voice.
>
> And the night shall be filled with music,
> And the cares that infest the day,
> Shall fold their tents, like the Arabs,
> And as silently steal away.

It is not my purpose to deny that these lines contain important clues toward the comprehension of Longfellow's poetic faith and practice, nor yet that the sympathetic understanding of the humbler branches of the poet's art here expressed is profoundly characteristic of him. There are implications in the poem, nevertheless, which are less simple than they appear. For one, the reference to the poet

> Whose songs gushed from his heart
> As showers from the clouds of summer,
> Or tears from the eyelids start.

The whole doctrine of the character—or, if you prefer, the "psychology"—of the poetic inspiration, as expressed here, is important for the understanding of greater poets than Longfellow, and nothing could be more superficial than to imagine that we understand either what he believed or how he functioned in this area, merely having absorbed the surface meaning of the words here employed. The truth of the matter is that these lines do not formulate a creed; they merely express a mood. For the same man who wrote them also declared—and now he *was* speaking for himself:

And now I long to try a loftier strain, the sublimer Song whose broken melodies have for so many years breathed through my soul in the better hours of life, and which I trust and believe will ere long unite themselves into a symphony not all unworthy the sublime theme, but furnishing "some equivalent expression for the trouble and wrath of life, for its sorrow and its mystery."

In his later days, as we have already seen, Longfellow did not like the "new" poets, but in his youth he himself was a "new" poet, resting under the common obligation upon this group—to create, as Wordsworth observed, the taste by which they are understood. "To you must be allowed the merit"—thus Longfellow's brother Alexander wrote to him, upon receiving his copy of *Voices of the Night*—"of giving to these western shores a new species of poetry—the mental in contradistinction to the sentimental—the healthy, in opposition to the morbid." And if the modern reader rubs his eyes at this, or sets it down to family partiality, what shall be made of the related fact, pointed out by Professor Gohdes, that *"Fraser's Magazine*, in 1853, initiated its discussion of . . . [Longfellow] with a charge that might be levelled at the metaphysical poets of the twentieth century, namely, a tendency toward the far-fetched and the extravagant."

Taking Longfellow's work in general, one can certainly say truly that though he admitted and admired the charm and the value of obscurity in some kinds of writing, he did, in general, insist upon clearness and simplicity, himself eschewing all the advantages which depend upon the suggestion of deep profundities beyond the reach of the everyday reader or comprehensible only to a clique. As he was an impatient traveler, so was Longfellow an impatient reader also, and he always wanted everything said as briefly as possible. "One so often sees the muse painted up to her eyes and bedizened with false jewelry that it is a positive relief to meet her without her rouge and in simple attire." He disliked ponderousness and pretentiousness of all kinds; he even wanted his own books physically small. Inevitably, then, he believed that "every work of art should explain itself," and that if it required a commentary it failed as a work of art. "All prefaces, and the like, are like labels coming out of the mouths of people in pictures." He comes very close to Milton's criteria for poetry —"simple, sensuous, and passionate"—when he compliments Frederick Locker-Lampson upon his poems, telling him that they are "very elastic and full of life and of animal spirits, which are the leaven of life."

That was why he loved the ballads, "the gypsy-children of song, born under green hedgerows, in the leafy lanes and by-paths of literature—in the genial summertime." It was for this reason, too, that he praised the early English dramatists for their "peculiar simplicity and raciness," and called "the old writers . . . better thinkers than we are. . . . There is a directness and earnestness that carries you along with them. You walk in broad daylight." He summed up the combination of depth and simplicity which he valued in his translation of Tegnér's "The Children of the Lord's Supper":

> Friendly the teacher stood, like an angel of light there among
> them,
> And to the children explained the holy, the highest, in few
> words,
> Thorough, yet simple and clear, for sublimity always is
> simple,
> Both in sermon and song, a child can seize on its meaning.

But what of Alexander Longfellow's "the mental in contra-distinction to the sentimental"? *Is* not Longfellow, then, a romantic, a sentimental, a didactic poet? an idealist, a weaver of rimed moralities?

In one of the clearest, briefest, and most direct of his aesthetic pronouncements, in "The Singers," he gives poetry a threefold function:

> To charm, to strengthen, and to teach.

He did not believe that the purpose of the imagination was "to devise what has no existence, but rather to perceive what really exists . . . not creation but insight."

> By the mirage uplifted, the land floats vague in the ether,
> Ships and the shadows of ships hang in the motionless air;
> So by the art of the poet our common life is uplifted,
> So, transfigured, the world floats in a luminous haze.[1]

Actually, of course, there is only one kind of art that is "true to nature," and that is bad art. But there are degrees in this matter as in others, and no reasonable person would expect Longfellow to come as close to reproducing actuality as a realistic novelist does. He himself, certainly, owned no such obligation. As a matter of fact, he did not do it even when he tried to be a novelist, as *Kavanagh* plainly shows. Many poets, however, have been closer observers of life at first hand than he was. He had no first-hand knowledge of either the Acadian or the Western backgrounds of *Evangeline*. For the West he turned to Bonvard's panorama of the Mississippi, and he built up his idyllic picture of Grand Pré out of the elements drawn from various readings and his own travel. He made "the reef of Norman's Woe" world-famous, but he seems to have had only the haziest notion where it was. Neither, for that matter, was "the schooner Hesperus" wrecked there.[2] He did not bother to visit Plymouth before writing *The Court-ship of Miles Standish.*

In an early lecture on the lives of literary men, Longfellow himself distinguished between two "Schools of Poetry"—"the Ideal and the Actual."

The first endeavors to invest ideal scenes and characters with truth and reality:—The second, on the contrary, clothes the real with the ideal, and makes actual and common things radiant with poetic beauty.

Of the former are Byron, Schiller, Percival:—of the latter, Goethe, Wordsworth, Bryant. The former are poets of passion;—the latter are poets of observation, and reflection. I would not willingly compare these schools and decide between them; but rather admire what is excellent in both. Our feelings tell us which we prefer; and our feelings vary; and with them our judgment. At times our spirits need the stimulus of a bold, brave impulse:—at times, the soothing quiet of reflection;—and the poets of each class commend themselves to us according to the mood we are in. . . .

No doubt. But it is also true that the "Ideal" type of poet commends himself to us according to whether he idealizes in a strong way or a weak way. The "candid camera" artist gets "warts and all"; the painter may put the warts in or leave them out, but if he leaves them out, it will be because they are not germane to his purpose, and not simply because he does not think them "pretty."

Which did Longfellow do? He did the first, and he also did the second, depending upon whether we are considering his poetic practice at its best or at its worst.

His tendencies may be illustrated and the workings of his temperament observed in connection with his use of the past. Being a professional scholar, Longfellow knew, better than most poets do, that the past is not really more romantic than the present, but only looks so to us because it is farther away:

We see the tree-tops waving in the wind, and hear the merry birds singing under their green roofs; but we forget that at their roots there are swine feeding upon acorns. With the Present it is not so. We stand too near to see objects in a picturesque light.

Sometimes, however, he prefers to ignore such considerations, and simply surrender himself to the charm of the past:

> Dreams that the soul of youth engage
>   Ere Fancy has been quelled;
> Old legends of the monkish page,
> Traditions of the saint and sage,
> Tales that have the rime of age,
>   And chronicles of old.

So it was part of the charm of the Wayside Inn that it had become

> A kind of old Hobgoblin Hall,
> Now somewhat fallen to decay,
> With weather-stains upon the wall,
> And stairways worn and crazy doors,
> And creaking and uneven floors,
> And chimneys huge, and tiled and tall.

Longfellow admits—and accepts—his own romanticism in the very last poem he ever wrote, "The Bells of San Blas," where he speaks of himself as

> a dreamer of dreams,
> To whom what is and what seems
> Are often one and the same.

No doubt we often think of Longfellow in this aspect. We think of him, too, and justly, as the gentle poet of the domestic affections, but this does not mean that harsher themes and emotions lay altogether outside his range. If this had been true, the action-subjects to which he was predisposed through his sympathy for early and primitive peoples would have been impossible for him.

There is a suggestion of the power he was to develop in this field in the early "Burial of the Minnisink," but the power was realized more fully in "The Saga of King Olaf," in many passages of *The Song of Hiawatha*, and elsewhere. It is true that he combines the mythical (Algonquin or Chippewa) Manabozho with the historical (Iroquois) Hiawatha, but it is not true that the whole element of primitivism in his work is thus automatically cancelled out.

Moreover, his idealizing of the past was not all weakness. "Men do not love truth less, in seeming to love fiction more. They love truth because it *is* truth; and they love fiction, not because it is fiction, but because it resembles truth." As Longfellow saw it, man's need for mental excitement itself testified to his spiritual nature:

All animals, save only man, follow the laws of nature, without seeking to improve or refine them. But man must spiritualize them by a gloss, —by a voluptuous commentary. For him the impulse of the present is strengthened by the memory of the past and the anticipations of the future, and the desire is quickened by imagination, which casts its spell upon us, till the deformed seems beautiful, and the sensual is clothed upon with the ideal.

After all, to reproach a creative writer for being more interested in the past for what his imagination can make of it than for what it was objectively is to reproach him for being a creative writer. As a matter of fact, he values—and employs—the present in much the same way.

Longfellow understood the temptations of the romantic imagination, and presented them in the dreamy Mr. Churchill of *Kava-*

nagh. Like Hawthorne in the custom house, Mr. Churchill knows that native sources of literary material and inspiration lie all around him, but in practice he overlooks them, for to him the near always suggests the far. His basic difficulty, however, is not that he is enthralled by the past, but simply that he lacks the energy required to transform his dreams into literature. When a writer has such energy, when his imagination is sufficiently vital to be able to use the past so that it takes on fresh life in the present, then past and present have coalesced.

Longfellow did this upon many occasions. He did it with "The Village Blacksmith." The actual smithy described stood at the site still marked by a plaque, on Brattle Street, between the poet's house and Harvard Square, but in writing the poem, Longfellow intended also to praise his own blacksmith ancestor in Newberry. Again, Longfellow's very first poem, "The Battle of Lovell's Pond," took its inspiration from American history, and from his teacher Thomas Upham's earlier treatment of the subject. But the young writer could not bear to leave uncontroverted his predecessor's assertion that the heroes of the battle were to be forgotten. Instead:

> They are dead; but they live in each Patriot's breast,
> And their names are engraven on honor's bright crest.

For the past inspired a feeling of piety in Longfellow, and a desire to preserve whatever it had held that was lovely and of good report. He felt this even about his beautiful house, and the feeling saved from materialism his devotion to it and its contents: he served as a priest at the sanctuary, to hold the place inviolate because Washington had been there. Above everything else, his poetry is the utterance of a sensitive, cultivated man, brooding over and assimilating his past, and possessing himself of his moral and aesthetic inheritance.

Of course this eclectic quality of his mind did not manifest itself only in the way of assimilating or amalgamating past and present. Thus Bliss Perry once remarked of him that he preferred to enter the house of life by the library door. This was not primarily a matter of quotations and literary allusions; indeed he calls himself "an enemy to quotations." But he does use literature to clarify life; from his own limited experience, he appeals to the wider racial experience which has been preserved in literature. A village on the Isle of Wight is "all like a scene on the stage," and a drunken man suggests what Molière would have made of him. In 1826 the sick actor Talma "has been for some time hanging like Mahomet's coffin between heaven and earth." He realizes an actual storm by thinking of a storm in the "Inferno"; a real woman is memorable because she recalls the Blessed Damozel. The approach of the Civil War is described in terms borrowed from Greek tragedy. Longfellow even lends his own knowledge of Teutonic legendry to John Alden:

> "Truly, Priscilla," he said, "when I see you spinning and
>   spinning,
> Never idle a moment, but thrifty, and thoughtful of others,
> Suddenly you are transformed, are visibly changed in a
>   moment;
> You are no longer Priscilla, but Bertha the Beautiful Spinner."

Unless Priscilla was, for her milieu, a somewhat unreasonably bookish damsel, I should think she must have taken this as a somewhat doubtful compliment.

But it is not only the standard classical and European legend and literature which Longfellow uses in this way: he even draws upon his American contemporaries. He sees Jonathan Johnson spearing flounders on the wharf at Nahant, and thinks of Rip Van Winkle. He glimpses the "gray head" of Dr. Nichols through the study window, and immediately Judge Pyncheon pops into his mind. The east wind puts him in mind of Poe—"chilling and killing my Annabel Lee." Nor does he entirely overlook an American poet Longfellow, for a "bleak West Wind" of 1854 is called "the wind of Mudjekeewis," and when a nursing task is thrust suddenly upon his sister Annie, he compares her to Evangeline, "only something more and better."

Carl Johnson has remarked that Longfellow "was quick to see

parallels between his own feelings and experiences and those described in literature." He was not quick merely, but eager and pleased:

Have you remembered, or noticed, that the days and dates of 1864 correspond with those of the Dantesque 1300?—so that in both years Good Friday falls on the 25th of March. Five hundred and sixty-four years ago today, Dante descended to the *città dolente;* and today, with the first two cantos of the *Inferno* in my hand, I descended among the printers' devils—the *malebolge* of the University Press. Is it a good omen? I know not.

Once he told Mrs. Fields that if she would read Schiller's poem, "The Ring of Polycrates," she would know how he felt about his visit to her. He tells the children that they

> are better than all the ballads
> That ever were sung or said;
> For ye are living poems,
> And all the rest are dead.

Yet when his own children raid his study, it is a literary allusion which comes to his mind to clarify the experience:

> They almost devour me with kisses,
> Their arms about me entwine,
> Till I think of the Bishop of Bingen
> In his Mouse-Tower on the Rhine!

He turned to literature for an expression of his own feelings even in the blackest hour of his life, and I am sure Tennyson must have been deeply moved could he have known that the only comment Longfellow made in his journal when Fanny Appleton died was to quote a stanza from one of the Englishman's poems. On February 27, 1881, Longfellow recorded in his journal his penultimate birthday:

My seventy-fourth birthday. I am surrounded by roses and lilies. Flowers everywhere,—

> And that which should accompany old age,
> As honor, love, obedience, troops of friends.

Even in his last illness he writes of himself, "I know not whether I shall pull through, but I have as much hope as had the old bishop of Salamanca."

Longfellow's "sentimentalism," like that of other nineteenth-century poets, is not a very profitable subject for discussion now, for our own rebellion against the nineteenth-century softness in this aspect is still recent enough to disqualify us from evaluating it fairly.

> Silently one by one, in the infinite meadows of heaven,
> Blossomed the lovely stars, the forget-me-nots of the angels.

These are two of Longfellow's most frequently-quoted lines, endeared to many of us by a thousand associations of youth; but judged by absolute standards, they would have to be called sentimental in any period, for their beauty is that of a weak fancy, rather than a penetrating or clarifying imagination. Longfellow himself sometimes rebelled against just such sentimentality—in Silvio Pellico, for example, whose work would, he thought, have been better "for a blast or two of the North." But at other times he succumbs to it. He thinks it a high tribute that Felton wept over "Footsteps of Angels," and he himself created some of his poems—"The Reaper and the Flowers," for one—in a very tearful mood.[3]

The discussion of Longfellow's didacticism involves similar difficulties. To use art as a "vehicle" to convey a moral "lesson" is condemned in the twentieth century by everybody who knows what art is. On the other hand, we are quite as sure as Matthew Arnold was that literature is "a criticism of life," and it would be unreasonable to ask any nineteenth-century poet to differentiate between what we love and what we hate precisely as we should do it ourselves. Whatever may be said about Longfellow's successes and failures along this line, this much is certain: he was much less the didactic poet than he is often considered to have been.[4]

It is not only Longfellow's enemies who have misrepresented him on this point: sometimes he has been wounded in the house of his friends. In the Preface to his official biography of his brother, Samuel Longfellow has interpreted this matter in terms which make it quite clear that, though he himself wrote verses, he thought like a clergyman and not like a creative writer. As the biographer sees it, Longfellow viewed his art merely as an agency of uplift. There was no vital relationship between form and content. "His art he valued, not for its own sake, but as a vehicle for noble, gentle, beautiful thought and sentiment." Beyond that "not for its own sake," moral condescension toward art and artists—and complete misapprehension of the way art is created—cannot go.

Of course, this is not to say that Longfellow rejected the poet's teaching function. That much has already been made clear. In *The New England Tragedies* he resurrects the errors of his ancestors

> For the lesson that they teach:
> The tolerance of opinion and of speech.

But here the "moral" inheres in the subject, and is not superimposed upon it; this is what *The New England Tragedies* "mean"; and the poet could not have understood his own materials if he had failed to perceive it. But in any case we are not obliged to think of Longfellow as one who saw teaching as the sole end and aim of the poet's striving.

> And the Poet, faithful and far-seeing,
>   Sees, alike in stars and flowers, a part
> Of the self-same, universal being,
>   Which is throbbing in his brain and heart.

Many nineteenth-century poets were sentimental in their attitude toward nature. Nobody would accuse Longfellow of being unresponsive to natural charm and beauty. Portland's lovely setting, "rising beautifully in terraces above the sea," conditioned his mind from youth, and this was supplemented by childhood sojourns with relatives in the country. It is a little surprising to find him, in 1835, disappointed at first in Trolhättan Falls, because "there is no startling, awful leap of the waters from the brink of a precipice." He did not usually require such extraordinary stimu-lation—indeed he found Niagara "too much" for him—and his journals are full of his joy and satisfaction in the quieter aspects of nature.

Like other poets, from Chaucer on down, he responded with special delight to spring, and, like Chaucer too, he allowed spring to take him away from his beloved books. "Spring is no time to read books. Out, out into the free air, ye book-worms; revel in the sunshine, and thank God for the spring!"

Longfellow loved spring not only for itself but also because it marked the end of winter, which his abnormal sensitiveness to cold caused him to dislike. Winter, too, had its splendors, and as a lover of beauty he could not deny them—"the great oriflamme of day," for example, "blown up by the morning wind, and in its fields of gold a silver crescent and a silver star." As he walked across the bridge into Boston to go to the theater, he stopped to watch "the rising moon" shine "through the misty air."

The reflection of the stars in the dark water looked like sparks of fire. Stood still to hear the soft sound of the dissolving icecakes in the brine,—a low and musical sound, a gentle simmering like the foaming of champagne.

But this was no creative splendor, like the splendors of spring.

Spring always reminds me of the *Palingenesis,* or re-creation of the old alchemists, who believed that *form* is indestructible, and that out of the ashes of a rose the rose itself could be reconstructed,—if they could only discover the great secret of Nature.

Yet, if possible, he loved autumn even more than spring—the praise of October runs all through his journals—and autumn, too, had the power to draw him away from study:

Once more the ever welcome and ever glorious autumn. On the trees are no longer leaves only, but brown fruits. On the bushes are no longer blossoms, but clusters of red berries. And the wind has a rough manliness in its voice,—not the tone of a lover, but of a husband.

Naturally the birds and the flowers were important elements in Longfellow's delight in nature, though he knew nothing about either scientifically. Blanche Roosevelt says that his favorite flowers were violets, roses, lilies, and lilacs. About the lilacs at least there can be no doubt: he loved them so much that he hated to leave them long enough to go into Boston while they were in bloom. Everybody who knows anything about Longfellow knows about the "beautiful orange-tree, having upon it six oranges and a hundred buds and blossoms" which he bought one day in 1862 and took home and placed "under the shelter of a lemon-tree ten feet high, which for the last ten years has kept up a make-believe summer all winter long in my study." It filled "the room with its fragrance" and outlived him by many years. Characteristically, he wonders where the birds take refuge during a driving storm, and humanizes them, as he does again in "The Birds of Killingworth"; "they must sit in wet clothes" until they can sit "at the fireside of the great sun, tomorrow." At Uppsala, in 1835, he wrote a delightfully Dickensian description of the birds flying about "the old brick cathedral" as "the clergy of the feathered tribe."

Above all else, however, he seems to have loved the sea; "a never-ending delight," he calls it; and none of his other nature poems quite reach the level of those which deal with water.

The sea is Longfellow's deepest and most inclusive symbol [says Edward Hirsh]; no contemporary writer save Melville was more profoundly or constantly responsive to it. In Longfellow's poetry, the sea is the restless mystery of existence, and its unfathomable source; it is the energy of unconfined and subconscious life, and of liberty. In its effects, it is also paradoxical, merciful and merciless, purifying yet dangerous, at once death-giving and life-giving.

Even the flooding of the Charles by the tide was beautiful to him. And once he tells us specifically that he loves the sea better than "the imprisoning mountains" because "the idea of liberty is stronger there."

Like other nineteenth-century poets, Longfellow sometimes

reads ineffable meanings into nature and makes natural phenomena the symbols of human and spiritual reality. For him it is not only the evening star which

> Hangs suspended in the twilight.
> No; it is a bead of wampum
> On the robes of the Great Spirit,
> As he passes through the twilight,
> Walks in silence through the heavens.

In an early poem, he states the principle by which, in dealing with these matters, he was always guided:

> And the Poet, faithful and far-seeing,
>   Sees, alike in stars and flowers, a part
> Of the self-same, universal being,
>   Which is throbbing in his brain and heart.

So the tides image the passing of time. Flames aspire. Trees suggest the columns and ribbed ceiling of a great cathedral. Mont Blanc's avalanches are sermons, and her voice that of one crying in the wilderness. Nature brings holy thoughts to men's minds, and strength and solace:

> O star of strength! I see thee stand
>   And smile upon my pain;
> Thou beckonest with thy mailed hand
>   And I am strong again.

This is precisely the kind of thing that modern critics do not like in Longfellow. And in a measure they are justified, for many of the hortatory passages are weak and sentimental, attributing to natural forces spiritual qualities which they do not really possess:

It is raining now, late at night; raining gently,—a most Christian rain. Calm and holy quiet is around, and thoughts of the departed, the ministering angels who so soon unfolded their immortal wings.

But the objectors are less unassailable when they balk at such a passage as this at the close of "Songo River," where the stream itself is represented as saying

> "Be not like a stream that brawls
> Loud with shallow waterfalls,
> But in quiet self-control
> Link together soul and soul."

Whether this is good or bad is, I fear, merely a matter of taste. The nineteenth century liked it; we do not. And Longfellow's critics cut the ground out completely from under their own feet when they assume, as they often do, either that the poet's attitude toward nature can be completely set forth in the terms I have thus far employed, or that he would have been a much better poet if he had treated nature as the imagists were to do.

Incidentally he could do this also, and very effectively at times. Amy Lowell was once, perhaps apocryphally, reported as having declared that it was her mission to save the world from Longfellow. She ought to have studied "Kéramos" more carefully, and such lines as these from "Daylight and Moonlight":

> In broad daylight and at noon
> Yesterday I saw the moon
> Sailing high, but faint and white,
> As a school-boy's paper kite.

But the thing which it is important to remember, in comparing Longfellow with the imagists, is that he threw off this kind of thing like sparks from the flintstone; it never occurred to him that a man might make a creed of it, or stake his whole poetic reputation on it. For if nature has no *significance* for man—if it merely supplies him with materials to construct pleasant pictures, quite external to himself and his most vital concerns—then it can have no very deep significance for poetry either.

Thoreau was quite clear about all these things, for all his devotion to nature. "Man is all in all," he said, "Nature nothing, but as she draws him out and reflects him." And again: "If it is possible to conceive of an event outside of humanity, it is not of the slightest significance, though it were the explosion of a planet." The interpretation of life and the world as a unified whole, the reconciliation of nature and human nature in its manifold aspects

—this is the central problem of modern art, and the use of the symbol as a means of indicating or expressing it is perhaps the first technical device that comes to mind in thinking of artists whom moderns tend to value most highly. I am not among those who insist that all respectworthy art must have a serious intellectual content, but if we are going to apply such a criterion, then, so far as the question under discussion here is concerned, Longfellow must certainly be given a higher rating than the imagists.

In the over-all view, Longfellow's thinking about nature was neither wishful nor superficial. When he traveled through the Tyrol after Mary's death, he found overwhelming sadness in the mountains, but he was not so egocentric, even then, as to hold the mountains responsible for this impression; instead, he attributed it, correctly, to "my sick soul." He accepted no easy antithesis between nature and art. Sometimes nature seemed lovelier to him than any reflection or re-creation of it in art could ever be; a lovely landscape will make him wish that a painter were there. But why was it necessary to choose? "Art is the revelation of man; and not merely that, but likewise the revelation of Nature, speaking through man. Art preexists in Nature, and Nature is reproduced in Art." As early as the "Lay Monastery" papers of 1825 and his Commencement Address on "Our Native Writers," Longfellow speculated on the effect of scenery upon the mind, but nowhere, even in these immature works, did he commit himself to the thesis which Wordsworth has been accused of fostering—that spirituality and morality are somehow an emanation of the landscape. Thus early too he has discerned that nature cannot be depended upon to sympathize with man:

Our death brings no change to the face of nature. The woods and the waters are as green,—the skies are as fair, and the air as full of freshness and the trees of melody, as when we were on earth.

The early "Autumn Nightfall" makes the same point:

> The tree that shades the plain,
> Wasting and hoar as time decays,
> Spring shall renew with cheerful days,—
> But not my joys again.

And this is quite in line with the scene in the mature "Torque-mada," where the bigot's daughters are burned at the stake:

> O pitiless skies! why did your clouds retain
> For peasants' fields their floods of hoarded rain?
> O pitiless earth! who opened no abyss
> To bury in its chasm a crime like this?

In the nineteenth century a sentimental nature-pantheism was often made a surrogate for lost faith. Longfellow is quite free from all such obfuscations. "I love the works of Nature—but even more the works of man, 'the masterpieces of her own masterpiece'—as Goethe has said." When he visited Lausanne in 1836, he was interested, first of all, in Gibbon's house—"not that I love Nature less but Man more." His master Upham had never had any doubt that man, not nature, is the poet's theme. Neither had Longfellow, and it was thus that he escaped the romantic fallacy and enrolled himself proudly in the great Christian-humanist tradition. "Shall I thank God for the green summer, and the mild air, and the flowers, and the stars, and all that makes this world so beautiful," asks Paul Flemming, "and not for the good and beautiful beings I have known in it? Are they not higher and holier than the stars? Are they not more to me than all things else?" Even in the "Footsteps of Angels," with all its sensitiveness to nature, the real inspiration comes not from her but from the poet's dead friends and his dead love. In *Outre-Mer* and in *Hyperion*, and in the review of James Grant's book, *The Great Metropolis*, which is reprinted in part in *Drift-Wood*, the relative merits of city and country are debated at some length, but while the country is not slandered, the verdict is rendered at last in favor of the city. This is determined in part by the accessibility of works of art in the city, and the privacy which the scholar can find there, but these are not the basic considerations. For, "after all, what are . . . [the glories of nature] but the decorations and painted scenery in the great theatre of human life? What are they but the coarse materials of the poet's song? Glorious indeed is the world of God around us, but more glorious is the world of God within us."

Longfellow's considered utterances concerning the nature and function of poetry varied from time to time. I have no desire to make his formulation seem more ambitious or elaborate than it was, nor to dress it up in any currently fashionable psychological or critical jargon which might lend it a factitious impressiveness in the eyes of contemporary readers. Like all true poets, Longfellow sang spontaneously.

> As the birds come in the Spring...
> As the rain comes from the cloud...
> As the grape comes to the vine...
> As come the white sails of ships
>   O'er the ocean's verge...
> So come to the Poet his songs,
>   All hitherward blown
> From the misty realm, that belongs
>   To the vast Unknown.

So he wrote at seventy-three. It was true all his life. Experience came first, formulation afterwards. But for all that, there are complications in his theory of poetry; there are difficulties and apparent paradoxes; there are matters which need to be explained. And it may be well to seek the clue to these in his poetic hiatus of 1826-37.

This cessation of poetic activity has puzzled many students of Longfellow's life and work, including his grandson, Henry Wadsworth Longfellow Dana, who once remarked to Robert Stafford Ward that these very years (*aet.* nineteen to thirty) are the ones in which many poets do much of their greatest work: would Longfellow have become a greater poet, he wondered, if he had not lost these years? "With regard to poetry," Longfellow writes Caroline Doane from Portland, in March 1826, "I have not stopped writing, but I have stopped publishing, for certain reasons which I cannot go into at length in a letter." Writing to George Bancroft from Auteuil, August 20, he goes further: "I grow daily more certain of the fact,—that when I left my native land I left with it whatever little poetical inspiration Heaven had blessed me with."

Three years later, he wrote his sister Elizabeth from Göttingen:

My poetic career is finished. Since I left America, I have hardly put two lines together. I may indeed say, that my muse has been sent to the House of Correction—and her last offspring were laid at the door of one of those Foundling Hospitals for poor poetry—a New Year's "Souvenir."

Even after he has settled down at Bowdoin he tells Greene, "If I ever publish a volume, it will be many years first. Indeed, I have such an engrossing interest in the studies of my profession that I write very seldom except in connection with those studies." It was not until five more years had passed, and he found himself in Europe again, that he noted in his Danish journal having

Sat up late at night writing poetry—the first I have written for many a long, long day. Pleasant feelings of the olden time came over me; of those years when as yet a boy, I gave so many hours to rhymery! I wonder whether I am destined to write anything in verse that will live?

But even this turned out to be a trial balloon.

Lawrance Thompson has conjectured that Longfellow was discouraged about the quality of his early poetry (as well he might have been), in view of the comments that had been made upon it by Theophilus Parsons and his own father. Scudder and some of the other earlier interpreters of Longfellow threw out penetrating hints here and there. But Robert Stafford Ward is the scholar who has made the most determined and successful attempt to think through the problems involved.[5]

It is noteworthy that even in the renunciatory utterances just quoted, Longfellow does not seem at all out of sorts with poetry itself. There are simply obstacles in the way of continuing his poetic career now. When, in 1832, in the midst of the hiatus, he was asked to give the Phi Beta Kappa poem at Harvard, he was even "flattered that the committee of the Society should have thought of me as Poet."

Ward suggests, accordingly, that Longfellow never really intended to give up poetry permanently. He was merely postponing further composition in accordance with a well-laid and carefully prepared plan which he had worked out under the influence of the Swiss historian Jean Charles Sismondi and others. "With his increasing preoccupation with careful preparation and finished style, it is likely that he became concerned lest inferior work jeopardize his literary future. It seems clear that the cessation was due to his literary theories."

When Longfellow first encountered Sismondi is not known. He refers to him, however, in his first Inaugural Address at Bowdoin and also in his article on the French language in *The North American Review* for April 1831. But Sismondi was not the only influence in the direction indicated. Ward stresses that of Giovanni Vico also, with his cyclical theory of history, likewise reflected clearly, he thinks, in the Inaugural Address.

Moreover, before he encountered either Vico or Sismondi, Longfellow had come under the influence, at Bowdoin, of Thomas Cogswell Upham, whose ideas appear in many aspects of his poetic theory and practice. Like Longfellow, Upham was antimaterialist. Like Longfellow's own, his temperamental bias was away from metaphysical speculation and in the direction of what was later to be called pragmatism. The early Longfellow may well reflect him in being more inclined than the later Longfellow was to insist upon the use of American themes in poetry. But more important than any of this were Upham's views on the cultivation of the poet's talent. Upham saw genius as an inherited trait and believed the human heart the most important object of a poet's study. But he also believed that in the nineteenth century no poet could be what is commonly called "original." Innate talent must be assumed, but it could not be relied upon by itself. On the contrary, the poet must cultivate his gift by study and learning and practice of the most rigorous sort.

Professor Ward insists that Longfellow's letter to Elizabeth, which has already been quoted, is not out of line with this interpretation of the poet's intentions:

The first part of his literary career was to be in prose, as it was for the ensuing decade. But his studies had been largely in the history of poetry, and he had been translating. Translation was to occupy him, too, during the decade of prose composition. These facts are consistent with, not an abandoned, but a deferred project for a poetic career. It was, indeed, deferred until after he had subsumed in his experience the literatures of Northern Europe as well as the Romance ones. In its "House of Correction" his muse was engaged in the "hard labor" of translation.[6]

Why Longfellow spent so much time as he did in making translations [7] may seem clearer in the light of these considerations. If translation was not an essential part of his career, at least it must be called a wholly natural part of it. And whatever exceptions may be taken to his translation of this poem or that,[8] nobody has ever doubted his general skill or his amazing range as a translator. "Most readers," he wrote Freiligrath in 1847, "have not the slightest notion of the thought and real creative power that goes into a translation." More significantly, he had already reported to the same correspondent that translation was "like running a ploughshare through the soil of one's own mind; a thousand gems of thought start up ... which otherwise might have lain and rotted in the ground." And for his kind of poet, and with his training and convictions, it could hardly have been otherwise.

He stated his ideal in his translation of Manrique's *Coplas* in 1833: "The great art of translating well lies in the power of rendering literally the words of a foreign author while at the same time we preserve the spirit of the original." But at this time he was still willing to allow the translator the occasional use of "slight and judicious embellishments." "So I have occasionally used the embellishment of an additional epithet or more forcible turn of expression." By the time he came to his translation of *The Divine Comedy* he had changed his mind about this.

When he undertook to translate *The Divine Comedy*, which is in *terza rima*, a difficult form in English, Longfellow had to make up his mind whether or not to sacrifice "the beautiful rhyme that blossoms all along the lines like honeysuckle on a hedge," and decided that he must do this "in order to retain something more precious than rhyme; namely, fidelity, truth,—the life of the hedge itself." "The only merit my book has," he wrote Robert Ferguson in 1867, "is that it is exactly what Dante says, and not what the translator imagines he might have said if he had been an Englishman." To John Neal he was even more emphatic:

A great many people think that a translation ought not to be too faithful; that the writer should put *himself* into it as well as his original; that it should be Homer and Co., or Dante and Co.; and that what the foreign author really says should be falsified or modified, if thereby the smoothness of the verses can be improved. On the contrary I maintain . . . that a translator . . . should hold up his right hand and swear to "tell the truth, the whole truth, and nothing but the truth."

Those who admire Longfellow's Dante praise him for having achieved just this; others complain that he was too unimaginative and mechanical, or that he was too mild a spirit to catch the power and fire of Dante, and sometimes they echo Howells's complaint that he translated Dante "into the English dictionary rather than the English language." But there is no serious question anywhere that his translations and his creative work were the products of a single mind. One could not change either without changing him.

The genuineness of Longfellow's poetic gift shows convincingly, I think, in the fact that not even such convictions and methods of working as have been outlined here ever robbed him of his inspiration, or, if you prefer, of his facility.

As the ink from our pen, so flow our thoughts and our feelings
When we begin to write, however sluggish before.

The Baron tells Paul Flemming that "what we call miracles and wonders of art are not so him who created them, for they were created by the natural movement of his own great soul."

Of "The Wreck of the Hesperus," written in its first form at a sitting, immediately after the idea had entered his mind (an excellent example of what Henry James calls "the suddenly-determined absolute of perception"), Longfellow records that it came not by lines but by stanzas. "The Arrow and the Song" was jotted down under a similar sudden inspiration one Sunday morning before church. Of "Blind Bartimeus" he sends this interesting account to Sam Ward:

> I was reading this morning, just after breakfast, the tenth chapter of Mark, in Greek, the last seven verses of which contain the story of blind Bartimeus, and always seemed to me remarkable for their beauty. At once the whole scene presented itself to my mind in lively colors, —the walls of Jericho, the cold winds through the gate-way, the ragged, blind beggar, his shrill cry, the tumultuous crowd, the serene Christ, the miracle; and these things took the form I have given them above.

Longer works, too, were often produced, once they had got under way, with great rapidity: "The Saga of King Olaf" in little more than fifteen days, "Judas Maccabeus" in eleven, *The Divine Tragedy* in less than a month. "If I had a hundred hands, I could keep them all busy with *Hiawatha*. Nothing ever absorbed me more." For thirty-four successive days, he translated a canto of the "Inferno" every day.

That, of course, was when the full force of his inspiration was upon him, when he knew the truth of what he wrote in "The Poets," that the glory not of recognition but of achievement eclipses, for the artist, all his pains:

> Yes; for the gift and ministry of Song
> Have in them something so divinely sweet,
> It can assuage the bitterness of wrong;
> Not in the clamor of the crowded street,
> Not in the shouts and plaudits of the throng,
> But in ourselves, are triumph and defeat.

"I have thought all the while"—so he writes Colin Grant Mackenzie, thanking him for the gift of his poems—"what a blessing it must be to you, as it is to any one, to possess this gift of song, so as to set toil to music, and to turn the routine of daily life into verse."

But it was not always like that. If it could be, then, as Shelley observed, "man"—or at least the artist—"were immortal and omnipotent." There were times when it would not come at all—"Tried to work at Evangeline. Unsuccessful"—or when an interruption would break up the writing mood and make it impossible to recover: "One bad effect the visit to East Greenwich had; it broke up entirely my poetic mood, and I cannot bring it back again. Any change produces this effect. The mind whirls off in a new direction; and there is no astronomy can calculate its return."

Moreover, even his rapid writing had often required long years of rumination behind it. The *Christus*, conceived in 1841, was not completed until 1873. "The great theme of my poem haunts me ever," he writes in 1851, "but I cannot bring it into act." "Judas Maccabeus" was not written down until more than twenty years after the idea had been conceived. "His especial interest in the American Indian and Miles Standish," observes Carl Johnson, "dates from 1823, but *Hiawatha* was begun only in 1854 and *The Courtship of Miles Standish* in 1857." Even with short poems, the expression of the idea did not always follow immediately upon conception. "I have had an idea of this kind in my mind for a long time," he observes of "The Reaper and the Flowers." "This morning it seemed to crystallize at once, without any effort of my own."

"Crystallize" is the key word here. Properly understood, it indicates the combination of spontaneity and careful craftsmanship which Longfellow achieved.[9] "My poetry . . . is written seldom; the Muse being to me a chaste wife, not a Messalina to be debauched in the public street." And he adds, to Sam Ward, in 1839: "Your idea of mental *crystallization* is fine."

One would expect such a writer as Longfellow to revise carefully. As a matter of fact, he revised with reasonable care, but he was not an extremist. Nor was he forever reworking his poems, like Poe or Walter de la Mare. He himself says of *Evangeline* that the portions which he wrote in the morning at his standing desk required no revision. Yet we know that he submitted *Evangeline* unpublished to three friends—Sumner, Folsom, and Felton—and went over their suggestions with great care. He liked best to revise in proof—a luxury which few modern authors can afford. "It brings it out clearer to see it in print; the mazes of manuscript are obscure and perplexing." What revision he did make was always neat and thorough.[10]

By the same token, one would not expect such a writer as I have been describing to be much given to occasional poetry, and again Longfellow runs true to form. Of one social affair, in 1858, he records that "both Holmes and Lowell read poems: the first, serious; the second, humorous, and both good. I contributed nothing by my 'august presence.'" In this matter of response to external stimulation, he stood at the opposite pole from Holmes, and when George William Curtis begs him for a national song, he comments, "I am afraid the 'Go to, let us make a national song,' will not succeed. It will be likely to spring up in some other way." In 1848 Samuel Longfellow wrote to Fanny, asking her whether she thought Henry could be persuaded to write a hymn for his ordination. "I should be most glad to have it, but have not asked him, knowing his little inclination for that kind of composition." He wrote the hymn, and a good one too, but he was unable to produce another, ten years later, for the dedication of Sam's new church in Brooklyn, having "just written one for the new College Chapel," and being unable consequently to find anything "more to say on the topic." When, in 1848, he was asked to provide a poem to celebrate Boston's new source of water supply, he chose instead to scribble some burlesque verses for his own amusement.[11]

The brilliant exception is, of course, the "Morituri Salutamus," one of his most distinguished poems.

After telling my classmates that I could not write a poem for their Fiftieth Anniversary, I have gone to work and written one; some two or three hundred lines in all, and quite long enough. Whether I shall have the courage to read it in public, when the time comes, is another question.

What happened here, as in the case of his few other successful occasional poems—"A Ballad of the French Fleet," for example, which was written to save the Old South Meeting House, or "The Three Silences of Molinos," for Whittier's seventieth birthday—was that a suggestion from the outside had dropped into his inner consciousness and come to life there. His trouble had never been that he could not take *suggestions*, for he was not the self-centered or autobiographical kind of poet: none was ever less so. The point is simply that he could not create to order: his muse would not be forced.

There is no better illustration of the way inner and outer coalesced in his imagination than is afforded by the circumstances under which he wrote his touching poem in memory of his dead wife, "The Cross of Snow." This is one of his few personal utterances, and it is the most intensely, poignantly personal of them all —so much so, indeed, that he never published it, but left it to be found among his papers and published by others after his death. Yet it took its point of departure—and its central image—from a picture of the actual cross in "a book of Western scenery" which he chanced to examine, and it might never have been written at all if he had not encountered that picture and found his imagination stimulated by it. Longfellow always felt much more comfortable when a suggestion came to him in this casual way than he did when somebody came along and said, "Look, here is something you ought to write a poem about."

This is a part of the curious independence of his character, which is all the more striking because of his extraordinary gentleness. Longfellow fulfilled the Blakian or Shavian ideal of the virtuous life, as Shaw has expounded and illustrated it in *Caesar and Cleopatra:* he lived spontaneously, lived out from the center of his being, and all he said and did was the expression of his own nature. I doubt that he ever did anything that he did not wish to do, or that was in any way foreign to him, in response to public pressure. If he was on the conventional side, the reason is that his own nature inclined him in that direction, and not because he had forced himself into a mould to please somebody else. Similarly, he achieved world-wide popularity without in any way seeking it, and without modifying his characteristic literary product one iota for the sake of achieving it. Like the Bowdoin undergraduate, the famous author of *Hiawatha* and *The Courtship of Miles Standish* still looked in his heart to write.

These tendencies appear too in connection with a matter which has already been spoken of: Longfellow's persistent use of English hexameters in spite of the ridicule of his enemies and the serious doubts of his friends. He made this experiment in an age less sympathetic toward literary experimentation than our own and much more generally familiar with the classical tradition. But he never weakened or shifted his ground. Sending *Evangeline* to Barry Cornwall, he wrote:

I hope you will not reject it on account of the metre. In fact, I could not write it *as it is* in any other; it would have changed its character entirely to have put it into a different measure. Pray agree with me, if you can, on this point.

He even told the Duke of Argyll that Homer would never be properly translated into English except in hexameters.[12]

Longfellow's conventionalism in other aspects can easily be overstressed also, and often has been by his posterity. If he seems to us a "safe" person, the reason is less that he walked obediently in the paths his predecessors had marked out for him, without ever glancing over the fence into Bypath Meadow, and more that he established his rebellions and departures with such complete success that it is difficult for us to realize there was ever a time when they needed establishing. There was an element of pioneering in even attempting to live the life of a creative writer in Longfellow's time.[13] He pioneered when he rejected the law as an ad interim method of earning a living and turned instead to teaching not the classics but rather the then novel and, educationally speaking, comparatively unestablished modern languages. Even the uninitiated can still perceive the element of pioneering involved in his use of native American materials in *Hiawatha* and other poems, but only a specialist in early American literature grasps the full force of Van Wyck Brooks's remark that his first published book, the translation of Manrique, "an act of high talent, if ever there was one,—sounded like full summer in its music, beside the pallid poems of the 'thirties." In the 'forties, Longfellow's closest literary advisers saw "The Skeleton in Armor" as too daring a departure from previous American didacticism in poetry; later, a Boston paper lamented his use in *Hiawatha* of "the silly legends of the savage aborigines. His poem does not awaken one sympathetic throb; it does not teach a single truth. . . . In verse it contains nothing so precious as the golden time which would be lost in the reading of it." And even in 1882, which was the year Longfellow died, the admiring F. H. Underwood was still confessing that he found *The New England Tragedies* "too depressing and painful."

II

Longfellow's place in the history of American poetry is something apart from the consideration of his aesthetic quality as such. Persons committed to the thesis that there was no "American" poetry before Whitman always make much of the idea that Longfellow was beglamoured of Europe and of the past. This notion is not of recent origin; neither has its expression been confined to Longfellow's detractors. He himself anticipated it when he had the Baron tell Paul Flemming that his attitude toward Europe was like that of a man who falls in love with his grandmother. "It is the past that shines in the eyes of Longfellow," declared Felix Adler at the time of his death. "In him the spirit of America, ere it set out to create the glories of the future, has turned back once more to revisit, as in a dream, the mystic splendors of the past."

Longfellow was indeed a passionate pilgrim long before Henry James. "I, too, in a certain sense, have been a pilgrim of Outre-Mer; for to my youthful imagination the Old World was a kind of Holy Land." Europe was the past, and the past seduced him even in his own country—what there was of it. "Nahant is very charming," he records in his journal. "I like it all the better for being haunted with ghosts."

But Europe was more than the past. Europe was also culture. As early as Christmas 1823, Longfellow writes his mother a letter from Brunswick, Maine, strongly expressing the feeling that he inhabits a backwater. He has been wishing himself in England all day long, he says. And he adds that he does not understand how anyone can read the fifth number of *The Sketch Book* and feel otherwise.

Actual contact with Europe did not blur these feelings. "The only consolation I have," says the young Bowdoin professor of 1829, "is that at some future day I shall be forced to go back to Europe again for nobody in this part of the world pretends to speak anything but English—and some might dispute them even that prerogative." Even later, at Harvard, "Visions of St. Wolfgang and other Tyrolean Lakes float before my imagination, a pleasing mirage in the great Prairie of a teacher's life." And he writes Norton, in Italy: "I made a great mistake in not staying longer in Europe. You were wiser, and have your reward."

Yet even with the very young man it was not all eager response. There can, of course, be no question about his complete capitulation to Spain. The enraptured attitude reaches its climax in his passionate apotheosis of Granada and was later recalled in tranquility in the poem "Castles in Spain." On the other hand, his first reactions to France were decidedly unsympathetic, and even on his second journey he regarded Paris much as a monkish writer might view a charmingly seductive woman. When he first saw Italy, it only made him wish himself back in Spain; later Naples and Venice captured him, and he calls the latter "the most wonderful city I ever beheld." Germany he says comparatively little about, considering how important German literature became to him, and he has a number of harsh words for both the Dutch and the Swedes. He is often very critical of England also, and in 1842 he had a bad attack of what he himself describes as "*anti-English* spleen." Naturally the Civil War did not help this.

But even when Longfellow was pleased with Europe, he carried an American yardstick in his head as a standard of measurement. "The Rhine is a noble river, but not so fine as the Hudson," and the Arno is only "a stream of muddy water, almost entirely dry in summer." He admits that the Guadalquivir is "more majestic" than the Hudson, and that it flows through a more fertile country, but it lacks "those happy-looking villages which are scattered along the Delaware." He sees nothing in Europe to compare with the White Mountains, and though he praises Spanish women, he is "proud to say that American beauty outshines them all." I do not think it an exaggeration to say that as a poet he used Europe much as he used his scholarship. Barrett Wendell is reported to have remarked that Longfellow "was too much of a poet to be a great scholar—and too much of a scholar to be a great poet." This is one of those flip epigrams that sound very well but generally mean nothing. There is no evidence that Longfellow ever confused the aims or the respective merits of scholarship and creative writing.

Like Wordsworth, he acknowledged the poet's obligation to general, not specific, truth:

> Nor let the Historian blame the Poet here,
> If he perchance misdate the day or year,
> And group events together, by his art,
> That in the Chronicles lie far apart;
> For as the double stars, though sundered far,
> Seem to the naked eye a single star,
> So facts of history, at a distance seen,
> Into one common point of light convene.

His practice was in harmony with his theory. *The Song of Hiawatha* reveals a poet's appreciation and realization of Indian and primitive ways, not an anthropologist's knowledge. The poet prevails; the anthropologist goes under; and the telescoping of Hiawatha and Manabozho remains to plague the specialist. "Paul Revere's Ride" is not a trustworthy account of what happened

> On the eighteenth of April, in Seventy-five.

It has merely supplanted what really happened in the public mind and memory, a striking illustration of how much more vital and important to mankind poetry is than history. The skeleton at Newport may well have been that of an Indian rather than a Norseman, and Longfellow was well aware of this, and not in the least concerned. He merely remarks that the Norse hypothesis "is sufficiently well established for the purpose of a ballad," as indeed it was. "Torquemada" takes an event which occurred during Philip II's reign and puts it back into the time of Ferdinand and Isabella. The Moravian "nuns" were not really nuns at all, nor did they live surrounded by any of the picturesque properties Longfellow supplied them with. The banner which they made for Pulaski was a small flag to attach to a lance, not a "martial cloak and shroud." And so it goes; instances might be multiplied indefinitely.

Longfellow's first important formulation of his views on Americanism in literature occurred in his Commencement oration on "Our Native Writers." Here he does not, "yet" at least, desire a literary break with England. "English literature is a great and glorious monument, built up by the master-spirits of old time, that had no peers, and rising bright and beautiful until its summit is hid in the mists of antiquity." And he recognizes, too, the difficulty of poetic achievement in a country in which there has always been a tendency to regard poetry as, first and best of all, a pastime. Nevertheless, he calls for an American achievement in literature "by those that have been nursed and brought up with us in the civil and religious freedom of our country." Our lack of scholarship he admits, and, apparently despairing of remedying it, he tries to make a virtue of it. The mere fact that "our writers will not be constantly toiling and panting after classical allusions" will throw them back upon themselves, upon the use of what they see and do not merely read about in books. "Every rock shall become a chronicle of storied allusions; and the tomb of the Indian prophet shall be as hallowed as the sepulchres of ancient kings." It is true that genius "must be born with a man"; nevertheless, "the influence of natural scenery in forming the poetic character" is not to be despised.

More mature in thought and expression is "The Defence of Poetry," which was occasioned by a new edition of Sir Philip Sidney's work, and published in *The North American Review* for January 1832. Here Longfellow anticipated much of what Emerson was to say five years later in "The American Scholar." [14] This essay begins with the familiar Longfellow protest against American materialism as the enemy of artistic achievement: "We are swallowed up in schemes for gain, and engrossed with contrivances for bodily enjoyments, as if this particle of dust were immortal,—as if the soul needed no aliment, and the mind no raiment." But the true glory of a nation must be sought not in her material endowments "but in what nature and education have given to the mind." Properly speaking, indeed, utility embraces "whatever contributes to our happiness; and this includes many of those arts and sciences, many of those secret studies and solitary avocations, which are generally regarded either as useless, or as absolutely injurious to society." It is true that neither poetry nor the fine arts will "till our lands," or "freight our ships," or "fill our granaries and our coffers; but they will enrich the heart, freight the understanding, and make up the garnered fulness of the mind." As for the common association of weakness and effeminacy with poetry and learning, it cannot stand in the face of such figures as Homer, Dante, and Milton. It is not "the necessary nor the natural tendency of poetry to enervate the mind, corrupt the heart, or incapacitate us for performing the private and public duties of life. On the contrary, it may be made, and should be made, an instrument for improving the condition of society, and advancing the great purpose of human happiness."

In this hour, the great need of the American writer was that he should be more "original" and more "national." Naturally this does not mean "that the war-whoop should ring in every line, and every page be rife with scalps, tomahawks, and wampum. Shades of Tecumseh forbid!—The whole secret lies in Sidney's maxim,—'Look in thy heart and write.' "

Properly speaking, a national literature is a literature that bears upon it the stamp of national character. To be American, poets must write "naturally . . . from their own feelings and impressions, from the influence of what they see around them, and not from any preconceived notions of what poetry ought to be, caught by reading many books, and imitating many models." For Americans,

skylarks and nightingales "only warble in books." They have no
more place in American poetry than "an elephant or a rhinoceros
[in] a New England landscape."

Longfellow can speak out in his Americanism on nonliterary
subjects also, though there is no chauvinism about him. He is
always honest about the failings of his country, and he can rebuke
her sharply when he feels she has disgraced herself. He could
even admit American shortcomings when they were pointed out
by others. But there was never any question as to where his own
heart lay or his loyalties were to be given. He did not consider it
proper for an American to accept a decoration from a foreign
government, and he himself refused one from even so liberal a
king as Italy's Victor Emmanuel. Writing to Louise Chandler
Moulton, he admits that an American may feel greater freedom ˎ
abroad. But he adds, "Please don't get expatriated," for "life is not
all cathedrals or ruined castles, and other theatrical properties in
the Old World." In 1847 he told Freiligrath that America was
apparently the only country *"where people have fair play."*

I think it may be said, then, that Longfellow champions and
exemplifies nationalism in literature, but it should be understood
that his nationalism is clearly of the eclectic variety. He speaks of
The Song of Hiawatha as his "Indian Edda," and it has been suggested that his descriptions of Acadia were based on what he
remembered of Swedish scenery. In *Kavanagh*, Mr. Churchill is
made to argue that a national literature does not have to be big
to match a big country; that it should not achieve nationality at
the cost of universality; that American literature does not imitate
English literature but rather continues it; that the development of
its national character cannot be forced; and, finally, that it ought
to embrace not only our English but also our continental heritage.

This is the kind of eclecticism that is exemplified by the Student
of the Wayside Inn:

> A youth was there, of quiet ways,
> A student of old books and days,
> To whom all tongues and lands were known,
> And yet a lover of his own.

Tales of a Wayside Inn is our best American poetic story book, but I think it less American than *The Canterbury Tales*, for all its use of material from foreign sources, is English. There is considerable discussion of the matter in the *Tales* themselves. After the Musician has recited "The Ballad of Carmilhan," the Poet speaks of it and its predecessors as all tales of the Old World:

> Flowers gathered from a crumbling wall,
> Dark leaves that rustle as they fall;
> Let me present you in their stead
> Something of our New England earth,
> A tale, which, though of no great worth,
> Has still this merit, that it yields
> A certain freshness of the fields,
> A sweetness as of new-made bread.

But the Student protests that he has no interest in where the wheat was grown:

> For if the flour be fresh and sound,
> And if the bread be light and sweet,
> Who careth in what mill 'twas ground,
> Or of what oven felt the heat,
> Unless, as old Cervantes said,
> You are looking after better bread
> Than any that is made of wheat?

The Poet's own tale is the aggressively democratic "Lady Wentworth," a "kind hearts and coronets" story. After it is finished, the Theologian, well-pleased, admits that the comparison to home-made bread was in order. "But," he insists,

> But not less sweet and not less fresh
> Are many legends that I know,
> Writ by the monks of long ago.

Later, the Student makes a similar comment on the Theologian's own tale of "Elizabeth":

> "A pleasant and a winsome tale,"
> The Student said, "though somewhat pale

And quiet in its coloring,
As if it caught its tone and air
From the gray suits that Quakers wear;
Yet worthy of some German bard,
Hebel, or Voss, or Eberhard,
Who love of humble themes to sing,
In humble verse; but no more true
Than was the tale I told to you."

Longfellow had no illusions about the superiority of European to American legendry; for the Indians, the White Mountains, and Acadia were already in his mind as subjects as early as the time he proposed his "New England Sketch Book" to Carey and Lea. Look at "To a Child" and "The Building of the Ship" if you wish to savor his realization of how complex the American heritage is; look at "Sands of the Desert in an Hour-Glass" for a good example of how intimately past and present were intertwined in his thinking.[15]

All the critics who have really understood either Longfellow or his times have been aware of these things. E. C. Stedman called his work "religious, in the etymological sense of the word, the binding back of America to the Old World of taste and imagination." Later, William Roscoe Thayer hailed him as "spokesman of the New American." "That New American is by inheritance a cosmopolite; it required a poet of cosmopolitan culture and sympathy to be his spokesman."

More impressive than these testimonies, however, are those of Whitman and of Henry James. Whitman's is particularly interesting, since it is by reference to his theory and practice that Longfellow has often been condemned:

To the ungracious complaint-charge of his want of racy nativity and special originality, I shall only say that America and the world may well be reverently thankful—can never be thankful enough—for any such singing-bird vouchsafed out of centuries; without asking that the notes be different from those of other songsters; adding what I have heard Longfellow himself say, that ere the new world can be worthily original, and announce herself and her own heroes, she must be well saturated with the originality of others, and respectfully consider the heroes that lived before Agamemnon.

Henry James goes at the matter in his own inimitable way, which is very different from Whitman's but quite as convincing. Longfellow, he says,

was perhaps interesting for nothing so much as for the secret of his harmony ... and for the way in which his "European" culture and his native kept house together. Did he owe the large, quiet, pleasant, easy solution at which he had arrived (and which seems today to meet my eyes through the perspective, perhaps a little through the golden haze of time,) to his having worked up his American consciousness to that mystic point—one of those of which poets alone have the secret—at which it could feel nothing but continuity and congruity with his European? I put the question—for all it is worth—without quite seeing how it is to be answered, and in fact merely as a manner of recording an individual impression of something in his liberal existence that was like a fine (in those days, at Cambridge, Massachusetts a delightful) ambiguity. If it seemed a piece of the old world smoothly fitted into the new, so it might quite as well have been a piece of the new fitted, just as intimately, into the old.

To have satisfied, in this area, two such antithetical spirits as Whitman and James would seem no slight achievement.

III

There remains one last question to ask about Longfellow as a poet. What was the motive behind it all? Upon what inner strength did he rely, and whence did he derive his aesthetic power?

His judgment of his own works varied greatly from time to time. In general he tended to think his poems better when he was writing them than after they got cold. His work on *Hiawatha* was interrupted by his fears that it might lack human interest. On the other hand, the final proofs of *Evangeline* pleased him, and he told his clerical admirer Murphy that *Evangeline* would outlive *Hiawatha* because it was more sympathetic.

He shunned personal publicity and objected to having his private conversation reported in print. He burned his first wife's journal for fear of its falling into other hands, and he even disliked the idea of the musical setting of "Footsteps of Angels" being sung in public. Yet he kept—and preserved—elaborate records of his own life, knowing well that many of them would ultimately find their way into print; there are even passages in which he explains himself to the hypothetical reader. Moreover, he knew that an author reveals himself pitilessly in his work. He never considered writing an autobiography, but he defends autobiographers against the charge of "excess and self-conceit." "In the lives of most men," he says, "there are many things which, if truthfully stated, partake of the nature of confessions, and tend rather to mortify than to flatter their self-conceit." Certainly his own *Hyperion* was naked enough, as the cantankerous Orestes Brownson pointed out when it appeared.

In the early days at least, it is clear that Milton's "last infirmity of noble mind," the desire for fame, had a strong purchase upon Longfellow. In the sonnet "Mezzo Cammin," written in 1842, he speaks of

> The aspiration of my youth, to build
> Some tower of song with lofty parapet.

But we are not limited to such evidence after the event. His boyish eagerness to write shows in the circumstances under which he rushed his first poems into print, in his youthful literary intercourse with William Browne, and in the way he began printing *Outre-Mer* even before he had found a publisher. "The fact is," he writes his father, on December 5, 1824, "and I will not disguise it in the least, for I think I ought not—the fact is, I most eagerly aspire after future eminence in literature; my whole soul burns most ardently for it, and every earthly thought centers in it." On the last day of the year, the same appetite is expressed even more strongly: "Whatever I study ought to be engaged in with all my soul—for *I will be eminent* in something."

It was Longfellow's own view that desire for fame died out of